THE BIBLE THEFT

OTHER BOOKS BY PETER SANLON

Plastic People: How Queer Theory Is Changing Us
(Latimer Studies) Latimer Trust, 2010

Simply God: Recovering the Classical Trinity
IVP, 2014

Augustine's Theology of Preaching
Fortress Press, 2014

PETER SANLON

THE BIBLE THEFT

GUARDING AGAINST THOSE WHO STEAL GOD'S WORD FROM THE CHURCH

CREDIMUS PRESS

First published in the United Kingdom in 2019
by Credimus Press
www.credimuspress.co.uk
Copyright © 2019 by Peter Sanlon.

The right of Peter Sanlon to be identified
as the author of this work has been asserted by him
in accordance with the Copyright, Design
and Patents Act 1988.

ISBN 978-1-79-205091-6

☩REDIMUS
PRESS

Dedicated with thanks
to David and Val,
who have contended for the faith
with spiritual joy.

Jude 3

Here is a series of penetrating expositions which are clear and contemporary, bringing God's changeless Word to bear on a confused and changing world. Such preaching has been called 'logic on fire' – some of these sermons are white hot.

A much needed message for today. Highly recommended reading.

The Revd Melvin Tinker,
Vicar, St John Newland, Hull

These sermons prepare a church family to stand by the Truth in a post-Christian culture. What I love about Peter's material is that it has already been tried and tested in the local church. It didn't go from desk to book, but from desk to pulpit to congregation to book. That gives it an integrity and a credibility which are to be cherished. So this material has already inspired and protected the flock. Peter wonderfully combines love and truth, faithfulness and pastoral care.I thoroughly commend this resource from the trenches of church life.

The Revd Rico Tice,
Senior Minister for Evangelism, All Souls', Langham Place

In a period of great turmoil in the Church of Jesus Christ globally, Peter Sanlon has given us a model of preaching which addresses the reality of institutional false teaching with great clarity, authority and sensitivity.

The sermons in this book will warm the heart and clear the head for effective engagement with the issues at stake in our current climate. They will also refresh those who are weary in the struggle.

The Revd Dr Liam Goligher,
Senior Minister, Tenth Presbyterian Church, Philadelphia

Contents

Foreword

I REMEMBER WHEN I WAS IN COLLEGE leading a small discipleship group for several high school young men. As part of the discipleship process, I had asked them to memorise a certain passage of Scripture so that we could all hold each other accountable on our Scripture memorisation.

The two young men quoted their passages perfectly and when it was my turn, I quoted it almost perfectly. I had added an 'a' where the 'the' should have been, and then in the next line added a 'the' where the 'a' should have been. I will never forget what one of these young high school students said to me chastising me for not quoting it correctly:

'All the devil has to do is get us off of the Word of God just a little bit, and then he has succeeded, because we have left the Word of God.'

It seems we live in a time when even in the Church people are not in sync with the Word of God. Yes, there have always been passages about which theologians, Bible scholars, and Church leaders have debated, but now it seems that what has always been the clear teaching of the Bible in theology and morality is being rejected as outdated, socially unseemly, and politically incorrect. Rather than standing on what the clear teaching of the Word of God says, these leaders are either now ignoring it or changing it to fit their needs.

What is the follower of Jesus to do?

1. Study the Word of God for yourself. Paul wrote to Timothy in 2 Timothy 2:15 'Do your best to present yourself to God as one approved, a worker who has no need to be ashamed, rightly handling the word of truth.'

2. Practise the Word of God in one's own life. Again, ponder Paul's words in 2 Timothy 3:16-17 'All Scripture is breathed out by God and profitable for teaching, for reproof, for correction, and for training in righteousness, that the man of God may be complete, equipped for every good work.'

3. Guard the Teaching of the Word of God. Guard it in your life, and guard it when you hear wrong teaching. Years ago, bank tellers in the US would study a dollar bill so intricately and thoroughly, that when a counterfeit bill would come along while they working at the bank, they could immediately tell it was a fake and guard the bank's interests. We, the people of God, should know the Word of God so well that when false teaching comes along, we know it is false, and then we can expose it and guard the teaching of the Word of God!

These sermons by Peter Sanlon are an excellent way to begin this discipline in your own faith journey. His teachings open up important passages which seem to be missing in many of our current cultural debates by Church leaders. Read them. Study them. Practise them. And then you will be able to guard the teaching of the Word of God.

Most Revd Dr Foley Beach
Archbishop of the Anglican Church in North America
Chairman-elect of GAFCON

Preface

LOCAL CHURCH MINISTRY involves an almost infinite variety of duties and responsibilities. All of them matter – team building, finances, pastoral care, liturgy. Yet it is my conviction that the unfolding of God's written word in Spirit-empowered expository preaching energises all other ministries and all other forms of word ministry.

When interviewed for the role of a parish minister I always quoted the words of Peter Adam, saying that I believe in 'a ministry that is pulpit centred, but not pulpit restricted.' I share these observations to underline for readers that the material in this book is a set of actual sermons, preached in an Anglican church in Tunbridge Wells in 2017.

Over the previous couple of years I made efforts to help leaders in our congregation appreciate the seriousness of the false teaching that has been spreading through the Church of England and the wider Anglican Communion. Numbers of people said that we needed to do something to bring the issues before the wider church family. A sermon series seemed fitting.

So a sermon series was planned which involved reading and pondering passages in the New Testament specifically relevant to helping us appreciate the seriousness of false teaching in the Church. I was worried that the impact of weeks of focusing on this would make us all feel depressed and sad. In fact it energised and empowered us. There was a sense of feeding on God's word and being formed by him into the congregation he wanted us to be. The sermons did not get into political or practical matters to do with Anglicanism – that was dealt with in business meetings and separate conversations.

For me one of the most powerful moments in those months was hearing the entire book of Jude read aloud as part of an Anglican church service. God's word has its own power when read publicly in front of people longing to hear from the true and living God.

Our congregation is made up of the normal wide variety of people present in our culture. We have people of all ages, classes and spiritual maturity. These sermons are not academic papers. They were prepared in the midst of pastoral visits, staff management and so forth. I usually preach at least three times on a Sunday and often have further speaking engagements midweek – so I am very aware that with more time these sermons could have been much better prepared. They bear many marks of being crafted in the midst of a demanding ministry and having been delivered as sermons rather than lectures. I speak from a very brief outline of notes, so these sermons were recorded in audio form and then transcribed by congregation members. I am very thankful to them for taking the time to turn them into a written manuscript.

I look back on this sermon series as a turning point for our congregation, and for my own spirituality. Our church as a congregation became more bold and convinced in the need to guard the gospel teaching. As a minister I was convicted that the Spirit uses his word to pastor, warn, unite and empower his people. I pray that in some small measure our experience may be yours also.

Peter Sanlon

The Revd Dr Peter Sanlon is an Anglican minister serving in Tunbridge Wells, England. He has researched and lectured on the areas of Doctrine, Church History and Homiletics and is also Director of Training for the Free Church of England. He is married and has two children.

Loving Clarity
to a Confused World

Romans 1:18-32

THE BIBLE'S TEACHING is what God uses to make us spiritually healthy: to give us vibrant relationships with God and other people. To grow as Christians the way that God would like us to grow. The focus of our series is a theme which occurs in almost every book of the New Testament – what it will require for God's people to be faithful to the words that God gives them and what it will mean for them to uphold and guard those teachings. Faithful churches guard the Bible's teaching because it is the key to people having good relationships with one another and with God.

One of the many areas of Bible teaching that is under pressure today is in the area of homosexuality. So this sermon is going to focus on that topic. The following sermons are not about that specific issue but about the general matter of what it means for the Church to guard and uphold the healthy teaching that God gives us - whatever the topic is that we face. But today we are going to look at this issue of homosexuality.

Many people feel uncomfortable with the idea of talking about homosexuality and sexuality-related issues in Church. There are a number of reasons for that which are very understandable. Some people, for example, think that we should not talk about sexuality related issues in Church because they are personal and private matters. If that's your thinking as we begin then do please be aware that it would not be possible, I think, to watch a whole day of television and not have the topic talked about! Are you aware that it is a matter of fact that children in primary schools in our area have been talked to about this topic in reception class – the very first year of entry into school? I have had parents in my study in tears about the sorts of things their children have been told by their teachers. They wonder, 'How can I as a parent help my child to understand what I believe God says in the Bible about the topic, when different views have been introduced so young and so early to them?'

Our culture is very enthusiastic about talking about these things. Even more importantly for us as Christians – the Bible talks about these issues of sexuality. We are looking at one of the longer passages that speaks about it: Romans chapter one.

Everything that God says to us in the Bible is for our good. God says things to us because he loves us. If God talks about something in the Bible, then we must be willing to talk about it and listen to what he says. It is not loving for churches or ministers to hide something in the Bible away from people. Some find these matters difficult for personal reasons; a friend or a family member is in a same sex relationship perhaps. There are numbers of people in our church in that situation. In a group of people as large as this it is inevitable that there will be some people that either right now or in the past have experienced same sex desires and attractions themselves. Whatever your personal situation it's important to say that all people are welcome to come into God's Church to hear and learn what God has to say to them in the Bible. It is not possible for me to say everything that would be helpful for every personal situation in one sermon, we would be here all day!

Whatever our personal situation we are always better off if we know what God says in his Bible and if we begin to put it into practice. This must be the case because God loves us and he cares for us. Some people think that the issue of homosexuality should not be talked about in Church because it's not relevant to them – I have been given two different reasons for that.

Some people have said to me 'There is no need to talk about this because it does not impact people at my age.' Or, 'I am sufficiently old that these matters are no longer really of importance to me. I'd like to just ignore them and let the next generation handle them.'

And I would say to people thinking that way, the Bible places a very high premium on the elders in our Church, the older people, in leading and setting an example for the next generation. Faithfulness to God is something that must be carried on right to the end of life. The younger generation who are very confused and really struggling with these issues look to the older generation for an example of willingness to uphold the biblical teaching even when it is difficult. They need your good example.

And then other people say, 'It is not really relevant to me because I do not experience same sex desires.' Well the Bible talks about these issues in order to prepare us for the future. Just because it does not feel relevant right now - we don't know what will happen in the future. It may well be that God brought you to Church today to hear this passage read and taught because he knows that in five or six years' time you are going to be put under intense pressure to compromise on what you know in your heart of hearts God says in his word. And this passage is here to prepare us for the future.

That is one of the great things that God does for us in the Bible. He does not just speak to us in the instant when we have a problem; he slowly feeds us healthy teaching so that we can build up the strength to deal with what occurs in the future. For all of us then, we need to work to understand and obey whatever God says in his word and that surely includes the topic of homosexuality. I recognise and understand that it is difficult and painful for many of us. So let us pray again as we begin. Let us just bow our heads and pray one of the great prayers from the Book of Common Prayer:

> 'Blessed Lord, who has caused all holy Scriptures to be written for our learning; grant us that we may in such wise hear them, read, mark, learn, and inwardly digest them; that by patience and comfort of thy holy word, we may embrace and ever hold fast the blessed hope of everlasting life, which thou hast given us in our Saviour Jesus Christ. Amen.'

We have **a confused world and a confused church** on this topic of homosexuality. Our world is confused. In the United Kingdom today we have two legal definitions of marriage which are not enforced in all the nations of the United Kingdom!

We have the legal definition of marriage as stated in the Church of England. That is the law of the land. The Church of England is the Established Church in England and as such, its laws are part of the legal structures of our nation. So the legal position of the Church of England as taught in the Canons and the Book of Common Prayer reflect the teachings of the Bible and they reflect the teachings of millennia of human culture – marriage is a relationship that can only be entered into by two people of the opposite sex.

There is a second and a more recent legal definition of marriage which is set alongside that in our country. It was brought in by the government a few years ago. It is called 'equal marriage' or 'same sex marriage' and this is a different kind of relationship which can be entered into by two people of the same sex. Despite calling one of these relationships 'equal' the reality is there are numerous differences between the two legal forms of marriage – both in the sex of persons that can enter into them, in the possibility of conceiving children and the grounds for divorce.

It is very, very confusing having two different definitions of marriage. I talk to people about that when they come to me for marriage preparation and ask them, 'Would it make a difference to you if the person you were about to marry was the same person but the same sex as you?' It opens up an interesting conversation about whether or not it matters that you are a man or a woman. It is very confusing that it is called equal marriage but when you begin to look into the details you find it has not been possible to mirror the traditional biblical vision of marriage.

There is no legal definition as yet of the consummation of a same sex marriage, neither is there any legal definition of adultery in a same sex marriage. It has not been possible for the Whitehall lawyers to find a way to pin that down in legal language which could be upheld in the courts and that will have significance for many areas of life. It's very confusing to discover that equal marriage is different to biblical marriage: two different definitions of marriage.

It is extremely confusing that Facebook in the UK now offers you seventy-one options to describe your sexual identity. Seventy-one options! Why so many? Because we live in a confused world.

Yet the Church is confused also, is it not? A lot of church ministers today are saying that the Church of England formally teaches one view on same sex relationships - but we are not really able to say that publicly because there are other people who take different views which are passionately held. These new views by default become equally valid and the Church moves from proclaiming the teaching in the Bible to talking about different views of what the Bible teaches. Proclaiming the teaching of the Bible is very, very different to discussing and exploring different viewpoints which may be equally valid.

The Church of Wales has issued prayers which churches can use to celebrate same sex marriages. The bishops say that churches are free to use them if they want. I have seen the Orders of Service that have been used recently. The bishops claim there has been no real change of teaching in the Church; it's just something they permit to happen.

Numbers of clergy in the Church of England are now in same sex marriages - in breach of their vows and the discipline of the Church of England. Yet little is done about it. A number of bishops in the Church of England have published books and articles opposing the teaching of the Church on marriage. They promised to uphold the Bible's teaching at their ordination yet nothing is done about it. All of this goes on while we are told that nothing has changed. A confused world and a confused Church.

When you turn to the Bible you'll find Romans 1 speaks at length about the topic of homosexuality. **God's word is not at all confused**. It is so very clear. It opens with a statement that is uncomfortable but we need to hear it: 'The wrath of God is being revealed from heaven against all the godlessness and wickedness of people who suppress the truth by their wickedness.' (verse 18).

The wrath of God is just the old-fashioned word for anger. God is angry at his world. Now we think that God should not be angry because he is loving and anger is bad, but actually the Bible teaches that God is perfectly loving and he is angry at things which are wrong. You think of the husband who's been married for many years and his wife finds out that he has had an affair and the wife is not the slightest bit angry or upset about it: there is no emotional response. Surely you would conclude that she does not care for her husband? That she does not love him because she is not angry at the betrayal?

The opposite of being loving is not being angry; the opposite of being loving is apathy, not caring.

God is angry at his world because he loves his world and he is rightfully angry when people turn away from him and ignore him. Now our anger is often, if not always, mingled with selfishness, pride and envy. But God's anger is selfless, humble and loving. He is a good God. The real surprise is not really that God is angry, but what he is angry about. We see that in verses 18-23. He is angry because people are confused about worship! Yes, God is angry because people are confused about worship. 'For although they knew God they neither glorified him as God nor gave thanks to him but their thinking became futile and their foolish hearts were darkened.' (verse 21).

'They neither glorified him as God nor gave thanks to him.' I visited one of our dear friends from Church in hospital this week. He was very weak; he was disorientated and he is very unwell. I held his hand and prayed with him. I was very struck and very moved that his prayer was one of unremitting thankfulness to God for his wife, for his Church, and for Jesus who died for him. It was profoundly moving. Thankfulness to God is one of the great marks of the believer, especially in times of suffering and sadness. When we give thanks to God like that man did in his hospital bed, God is being glorified because God is being put in His right place. God is God; he's in charge; every good thing I have I thank him for, because he gave it to me.

When we give thanks to God for all that we have, we are feeling ourselves to be dependent upon him. I am healthy today not because I was disciplined and went to the gym last week, but because he permitted me to take another breath of life in his world! God deserves my thanks. The language here is the language of worship. When we give thanks to God we glorify him as God. When we say he truly is God over our lives, we are worshipping him as we were designed to do.

You see it in the second half of verse 21: 'Their thinking became futile and their foolish hearts were darkened. Although they claimed to be wise they became fools and exchanged the glory of the immortal God for images made to look like mortal man and birds and reptiles.' The verse is saying that God is angry because people stop giving thanks to God, stop glorifying him and instead worship and serve other things in his creation. We live for things which God has made. We should say thank you to him for them, but instead we ignore God and get all excited about the things that he has made. The passage mentions the worship of physical things like animals, perhaps statues. I have visited countries in the world where people do worship statues: a little box outside the hotel room with a statue and little bits of fruit and money left there. The Bible calls that an idol. Something you worship which is not God. But you do not have to worship a little statue to be an idol worshipper. We can live for and worship a career, a family, popularity, control over others, comfort, sport, security from the savings in the bank, my reputation. Anything in God's creation can be worshipped and served and lived for. It can become an idol. It can be good things that God gives us.

We were made to worship the wonderful, loving all-powerful God but we exchange the worship of him for things in this world. We should thank him for them; not worship them and serve them. That is why God is angry at people in his world. We cannot say it is not our fault that we are confused. We so often do that at work saying, 'Oh, I didn't know – it is not my fault.' Verse 19 tells us 'what may be known about God is plain to them because God has made it plain to them. Since the creation of the world God's invisible qualities, his eternal power and divine nature have been clearly seen, being understood from what has been made, so men are without excuse.' So everybody knows in their heart of hearts that there is a God. We do not run to him; we suppress the truth and run away from him. I know that for many of us it's a surprise to find that God is angry; it is also a surprise to find that the reason for his anger is our confused worship.

What God actually does with his anger is even more surprising! In verses 24-27 we read of a world confused about sexuality, deeply confused about sexuality. Now if we were not really listening to the Bible reading from Romans 1 and we thought it was an opportunity to have a little doze, we might assume, would we not, that the passage teaches God is angry at things that people do? That God is angry at people for doing things he says are wrong in the area of sexuality? We might think that is what the Bible passage says. But that is not what the Bible passage says. If it did say that then we could read the passage and say, 'Well that is not something that I am involved with, so God is angry at those people over there but not me. I am better than them.' That would be totally bizarre.

For when you get to the end of the argument of Romans chapters 1-3, namely 3:9 and 3:19 you find the conclusion we have been building up to: God is angry at every single person in the world because all of us are guilty in various different ways. It would be totally bizarre for God to begin an argument that ends with that conclusion, with a big section which makes some people think he is not angry with them! No. In these verses we do not learn that God is particularly angry with an individual who engages in the homosexual lifestyle, rather we find that God is angry at everybody in his world for our confused worship.

What does God do with a culture which has confused the worship of God? He hands it over to be confused about sexuality. In other words it is not people engaging in same sex relationships that makes God angry; God is already angry at all of us for turning away from him. When you see a culture like ours which approves of homosexual relationships in a very deep way, you are not to conclude God is angry at them because of what they do. We are to see that there is the evidence that God is angry at me. God is wrathful at everyone because we have all turned away from Him to worship and serve things that he gave us. We do not give thanks to Him for all the good gifts he gives us, and that makes God rightly angry.

Let me show that to you in verse 24. 'Therefore,' you see that opening word 'Therefore,' teaching us what we're about to read is the result of God's anger at confused worship in verses 18-23: 'Therefore, God gave them over in the sinful desires of their hearts to sexual impurity for the degrading of their bodies with one another, they exchanged the truth of God for a lie and worshipped and served created things.' The idea is expanded in verse 26: 'Because of this God gave them over to shameful lusts, even their women exchanged natural relations for unnatural ones, in the same way the men abandoned natural relations with women and were inflamed with lust for one another.'

What are we to make of this surprising argument in the Bible? How the Bible is talking about the issue of homosexuality is not at all what we would expect; what should we make of it?

Firstly, this passage in the Bible, like every other passage in the Bible which talks about this issue, is crystal clear that homosexual sex is something that

God says is wrong, that his people should refrain from. There is widespread agreement among scholars of the Bible that this is precisely what the Bible teaches. So for example, there is a biblical scholar called William Loader who believes homosexuality should be celebrated and affirmed by Christians. However, he fully recognises that the Bible teaches the opposite of what he believes. In one of his books he mentions two academics debating on opposite sides of the argument. One of them is Robert Gagnon. He believes that the Church should not affirm homosexual relationships. The other one is Dan Via who believes the Church should celebrate same sex relationships.

William Loader quotes Via, saying this: 'Professor Gagnon and I are in substantial agreement that the biblical texts that deal with homosexuality, condemn it unconditionally.' Do you see how striking this is? These two different scholars on opposite sides of the debate - they both agree that the Bible teaches homosexuality is something of which God does not approve. William Loader himself goes on to comment that although the Bible is clear on the topic, the teaching of the Bible ought to be set aside and ignored by the Church today.

You see that is really the only debate to be had. The Bible is as clear on what God says about this topic of homosexuality as it is on any other topic of the Christian religion. It really is. The only debate to be had is whether or not God's people will follow, trust, obey, guard and uphold what God has said to them with his divine clarity. The idea that God does not know how to speak clearly to us is ludicrous, is it not? God invented speech. He is the all-powerful God. The Son of God is called the Word. God is able to communicate to his people, the only issue is will his Church obey him or not?

Secondly, it is very important to say that the argument in Romans 1 is not making the point that someone who engages in homosexual sex is worse than other people. As I have said earlier, that idea would undermine the goal of the first three chapters of Romans which is to convince us that all people are under sin and God's wrath.

One of my good friends, Sam Allberry, was a Church of England minister in Maidstone for quite a few years; he now works in Oxford. He is a man who experiences homosexual desires and seeks to uphold the Bible's teaching by not acting on them. He has written a very personal book in which he explains what the Bible teaches about homosexuality and what it means for his life. He can obviously speak about this in a personal way that I cannot. It is very striking what a short book it is! If I turn it sideways on it almost disappears it is so thin! The fact is that understanding what God says about homosexuality is not really a hugely complicated task. It does not take a long complex book. The real problem is that we find it difficult to obey God. Sam answers in this very short little booklet almost every question that the average person has about the topic.

Let me read to you a couple of comments he makes about Romans 1 which I think are really helpful: 'It is important to recognise in Romans 1 that Paul is talking in societal rather than individual terms. He's describing what happens to a culture as a whole rather than particular people. The presence of same sex desires in some of us is not an indication that that individual has turned from God more than other people or that they've been given over by God to further sin more than others. There is a parallel with suffering.' This is the helpful point he makes- there is a parallel with suffering. 'The presence of particular suffering in someone's life does not mean they have sinned more than someone suffering less. Rather the presence of suffering anywhere is an indication that as a race we are under God's judgement. Similarly, the presence of homosexual feelings in me reminds me that my desires are not right because the world is not right. Together we have all turned from God and together we have all been given over to sin.'

So where does this leave us? **A confused world needs a church's loving clarity.** The world is confused. The Church is confused. A confused world needs a church's loving clarity. In verses 28-32 we see a picture of some of the other sins that people are handed over to when they stop giving thanks to God in worship that glorifies him. There are many of them, they read not merely as a description of first century Rome; they describe my homeland in Ireland, they describe the city of London, they describe Tunbridge Wells where we live.

'Furthermore since they did not think it worthwhile to retain the knowledge of God he gave them over to a depraved mind to do what ought not to be done. They have become filled with every kind of wickedness, evil, greed and depravity. They are full of envy, murder, strife, deceit and malice. They are gossips, slanderers, God haters, insolent, arrogant and boastful. They invent ways of doing evil, they disobey their parents. They are senseless, faithless, heartless, ruthless.' (verse 28). Friends, that describes our world today. There are so many things that are wrong with us and with our world in addition to the glorifying of homosexuality.

That is the confused world we live in and the question for our congregation in particular and the Church of England in general is this: Faced with a world that is confused about sexuality, will the Church of Christ mirror back to the world its confusion or will we hold out to it the loving clarity of what God says to a world which is broken, hurting and lost? Will we mirror the confusion or will we minister words from God that have loving clarity? These are questions facing the Church of England today.

You look north and find the Scottish Episcopal Church has voted to change its marriage laws to mirror the confusion of the world around it. You look west and see the Church of Wales' bishops have said that at this stage we are not formally changing the marriage laws to mirror those of the world but here are some suggested prayers of celebration which you could use in your church after somebody's had a same sex marriage somewhere else. A number of those services have already occurred. That is the Episcopal Church of Scotland, that is the Anglican Church in Wales, and stuck in-between we have our much-loved Church of England. What will we do?

Well, the bishops will be revealing their plans, we don't know the details of it all yet. If it falls short in any way of the loving clarity of what God says in his word it will not just be a betrayal of the congregations up and down the country. It will not just be a betrayal of the liturgy and the doctrines that have been upheld in the Church of England for centuries. Much more seriously, it will be a betrayal of Jesus Christ who gave his life for the Church and if it happens that the leadership of the bishops of the Church of England falls short of the loving clarity that we find in God's word, then every minister and every congregation in the Church of England will have to decide: Will we join their betrayal? Or how will we ensure that the healthy teaching God gives us because he loves us, is guarded and upheld in such a way that we cannot be perceived in any way to be affirming things that God says are hurtful and damaging to people in this world?

For what we affirm as a Church and what we are seen to affirm really matters. In the closing comments of the passage we read that 'they not only continue to do these very things but also approve of those who practice them.' We need to take steps to make sure that our Churches are not seen to approve of things which God says we should not approve of.

I know there are difficult things in this passage, so let's remember that this is part of the Gospel message which is good news, and in Romans 1:16 the apostle Paul says 'I am not ashamed of the Gospel because it is the power of God.' Difficult though it is, these words are for our healing and for our restoration.

Lovingly Addressing Sin in the Church

1 Corinthians 5:1-13

WE HAVE TWO MAIN WAYS of dealing with problems in our relationships and problems in our dealings with other people when somebody behaves really badly - when they hurt us or when they sin against us, to use the biblical language. One way, which is very common, is to just disengage. We step away. If the problem has occurred in church we move to another church; if it occurs in the office, we avoid the person and quietly begin to look for another place of employment.

Another way we deal with the possibilities of

being hurt, or damaged by people, when they sin against us, is that we work really hard to keep our lives private. I have my private life, I am an individual and you have your private life, you are an individual. And by keeping each other at arm's length we make it (or so we think) harder for us to get hurt by other people's bad behaviour. And of course, we make it easier to hide the problems that we have, because if my life is private and individual, then you have no right to point out to me something I am doing in my life that might be hurtful or damaging to somebody else.

Disengaging from relationships when we get hurt, or trying to keep our lives very private and close to ourselves - these are the two main ways that people deal with their problems in relating to one another. When you come to read the Bible, you find that Jesus and the apostle Paul and God himself who is speaking to us through their words, are far more wise. When somebody becomes a Christian, they do not merely get a relationship with God; they get a relationship with all the other people who have relationships with God. Our relationships with one another in church are intimately connected to our relationship with God. And God knows that each one of us have problems and struggles. To use the biblical language: we sin, and God is realistic about that. He gives us other people in church to help us with that, and he uses us to help them. If, that is, we can turn away from those other unhelpful ways of dealing with relational problems – disengaging as soon as there is a problem, or trying to keep everything to myself as a private individual. If we can allow ourselves to be open to God's method of helping us, a really fruitful, joyful relationship with God and with other people in His church family, is on offer to each one of us.

Before we look at 1 Corinthians chapter 5, where we see one of the most serious examples of a problem being dealt with in a church family, I would like us first of all to see that the teaching Paul brings us here is nothing more than an application of teaching that came from Jesus himself. People sometimes think that Paul in the New Testament was the harsh, stern, legally minded person, while Jesus was the one who just said things that really were positive and pleasant. Actually no, Paul's teaching was absolutely at one with the teaching of Jesus, and you see that in Matthew 18, where sin in God's family is dealt with at the appropriate level.

Jesus teaches us that when there is some kind of sin or bad behaviour in the church family, it doesn't immediately move to the situation we read about in 1 Corinthians 5. If at all possible, it is dealt with quietly: one to one, or in a small group setting. Matthew 18:15 says: 'If your brother sins against you, go and show him his fault, just between the two of you, and if he listens to you, you have won your brother over.' And it is only if he doesn't listen that two or three of you talk together about it. That may happen on a number of occasions over a period of time. And only as a last resort, one may talk about it with the wider church family. Does it not show an incredible generosity and love and care of the human condition, for Jesus to say he knows that some things are embarrassing and difficult? You have treated somebody badly, and, yes, you feel bad about it.

So Jesus says if it *is* at all possible in the church family, let's try and prayerfully, graciously, deal with it in confidence. Don't go and announce it to the national media. Try to deal with it in a gracious and private manner.

It is very, very hard, to receive a rebuke well. It is also very, very hard to deliver a rebuke well! I have been in a situation where somebody has pointed out to me something I have done which is wrong, and all I really wanted to talk about is that the way they pointed it out to me was unkind. 'Let's talk about the way you have spoken to me. The tone of your voice. That is what we need to have a meeting with the church about. Not the thing you have talked to me about that I know I did wrong.'

I know how it feels – we are all the same. It is hard to have ourselves exposed, to allow people to speak into our lives, to help us change. It is also hard to do it. We are scared of saying something that somebody else might take offence at. But, friends, this is in the Bible, it is from Jesus. It is only if we allow this kind of mutual back and forth in our church relationships, that we can possibly have real relations with one another. That we can possibly grow and begin to overcome our sins and struggles, and have really good, positive relationships, not only with each other but with God himself.

It is scary, is it not? It has always been so. We think that our culture today is the first great individualistic one where we all want to keep ourselves private; but it has always been like this. In the Garden of Eden, Adam and Eve hid from God.

And we can come to church and really be hoping 'I can hide in church from God! I can just walk in, and sit here. Sing a song. Leave.' It has always been like this. St Augustine in the fourth century commented on this passage in Matthew 18 and said 'Your brother has harmed another, but by doing so he has harmed himself. If you ignore him, you are worse in your silence than he is in his abuse.'

Jesus wants us to genuinely love each other. At the very least that means we should try to make efforts to know each other. To have enough of an open relationship with one another, that we can actually see each other's faults. That if I am a gossip I should spend enough time with people that you see that I am a gossip and that somebody – please – would love me enough to quietly take me aside and say, 'Do you realise the way you gossip and talk about other peoples' problems, is really damaging? Could I pray with you about that?' Or if you begin to realise that there is somebody who in the way they treat somebody else in their family – perhaps a child or a marriage partner, is overly harsh and it is causing unnecessary friction and hurt. Somebody could take them aside and say, 'I know that you love your child and you are trying to do the best for them but, have you thought that perhaps you need to put an emphasis on gentleness and kindness? Perhaps we can pray about that?' Do we love each other enough to do that? Sin is dealt with at the appropriate level.

1 Corinthians 5 shows how this teaching of Jesus gets applied in one of the most serious types of situation; it's very rare and unusual, but it does happen. There is a situation in this church which is really serious. 'It is actually reported that there is sexual immorality among you of a kind that does not occur even among the pagans: a man has his father's wife.' (5:1).

It was a very serious breakdown of relationships. You can imagine the kind of chaos that is happening, as people take sides and as they argue; as they ignore or as they praise something that is very wrong in this church in Corinth of the first century. One of the first things that Paul says to the church in verse 1 is 'This terrible sin should produce grief not pride.'

He continues, 'And you are proud! Should not you rather be filled with grief and have put out of your fellowship the man who did this?' (verse 2).

If we do not have close relationships with one another then we do not even know when bad things are going on in marriages or lives or in families or in behaviour at work. If we do not have close relationships with one another it is all kept private. If we begin to get to know what is going on in one another's lives there is a temptation to turn a blind eye. Or even worse, as in Corinth, to begin to celebrate it and to say, 'Well here is a great example of a church being inclusive: here is a great example of a church being generous: here is a great example of a church being radical and taking brave steps to do things that are not normally done among God's people.' But Paul says in effect, 'No. When you look at these things going on you should be filled with grief.'

It is so sad that our feelings about what goes on in our lives fall far short of what the Bible says our feelings should be. I include myself in that. We think things do not matter and we casually move on. Yet God says that we should be full of grief and sadness at the damage that is done to somebody's life or family by people turning away from God's instructions in the Bible. Perhaps just reading this passage is a wakeup call to us that there is an issue in life that we try to ignore and push it down, when it should make us feel really sad. The grief should move us to talk to someone about it and to seek help from the wider church family. The sin should produce grief not pride.

In verses 2-5 we see that the tragic situation is treated by the church family with the goal being salvation. The situation is treated with the goal of salvation. Now the church family is told in verse 5 to do something that certainly looks most negative, 'Hand this man over to Satan, so that the sinful nature may be destroyed and his spirit saved on the day of the Lord.' What does it mean for a church to gather together in assembly to have the Lord Jesus present, as verse 4 tells us happens, and then to hand one of the members of the church over to Satan? It sounds quite extraordinary does it not? It has not happened in any of the services we have held over the last few years. What would a service look like in which this is done? For many years I have wondered that when I have read this passage. I have struggled to understand what it means to hand somebody over to Satan.

The apostle Paul talks about something very similar in his first letter to Timothy (1 Timothy

1:20). He writes in Ephesians about Satan being the 'Prince of this world' (Ephesians 2:2). When Jesus was tempted by Satan, the Devil said that he held in his power all of the nations of the world, and could give them to anyone he chooses (Matthew 4:8-9).

It seems that the Devil does have real authority and real power over this world. What does it mean then to hand someone over to him? I think I began to understand what is meant by that, when it was pointed out to me by somebody that the phrase Paul uses of handing the man over to Satan is actually alluding back to a comment in the Book of Job.

Job was a man in the Old Testament who had faith in God and trusted Him. And the Devil came to God, in the Book of Job, in the opening couple of chapters and said: 'Look at this man Job, he does not really trust in you, let me prove to you that he really does not have faith in you.' And in Job 2:6 God says to Satan, 'Very well then, Job is in your hands, but you must spare his life.' So when Job is handed over to Satan what it meant was, the Devil could do anything he wanted to him, with one exception - he could not kill him. His life had to be spared. So even as God handed a man over to Satan's power, God was still in charge. It is very clear in Job that Satan can't do anything that God does not allow him to do. He has to ask permission. God says 'Alright you can have him, but here is the limit of your power.' God still has a restraining force that he places upon Satan.

And we know also that God patiently allows people to continue to live in order to give them an opportunity to repent and come back to him (2 Pet. 3:9). That is His act of graciousness. And so when a man is handed over to Satan the protection that God puts over his people is removed with only one bit of protection remaining- the Devil may not kill him. So Paul says in 1 Corinthians 5, this same thing is to be done to this man as an act of last resort. As the only option left, as the final hope for him. If he is removed from the church, and he is sent out into the world, without the blessing and the protection of God, save over his actual physical survival, then perhaps whatever happens to him as he experiences the full horror of that, perhaps that will bring him to his senses. And like the Prodigal Son, he may come back home again to God. It is what happened to Job, perhaps it will happen to that man.

I have actually heard of a church doing this, by the way. This church had sent a missionary to another country to share the good news of Christianity. They paid for him, they sent him out after holding a commissioning service, and they began to hear that he spent his time living with somebody in an inappropriate way, spending all the money in a way that was inappropriate and not discharging his ministry in any faithful way at all. And so the minister and some of the church leaders went out to visit him, to talk to him, to pray with him, but he would not admit it. He would not change, he would not come home.

So they came back, they talked to the church, they read their Bibles, and, having several years previously held a Missionary Commissioning service for him, they held a De-commissioning Service, handing him over to Satan's ministry. With great love and with tears and with prayers that God would do good in the man's life, they held a service and they prayed together as a church family saying we are now doing what God told us in the Bible to do. We are handing this man over to Satan. We've done everything we can to bring him to his senses and he will not listen. And we now pray that as he loses the protection of God's people that you would preserve his life and bring him to his senses.

Obviously that kind of thing only happens in the most serious of situations. After many, many other options have been attempted. It is the biblical last opportunity for rescue. But note that it is done for a good intent. The goal is always good; whether you have a private conversation with someone you see behave badly, or whether there is two or three of you chatting with somebody, or whether it is this very serious final option, the goal is always to bring a person back to a relationship with Jesus. Therefore there must always be love, compassion, kindness, patience and generosity. To not be any of these is not at all loving. That is to allow people to hurt themselves, hurt other people and lose a relationship with God. But, if it has to be done, it must be done in a gracious, kind way, recognising that as I may help somebody else with a problem, I too need help with similar or different problems. None of us is better than the other. The goal is salvation and we all need help.

Of course, the temptation is always to ignore problems in our own lives and in other people's lives. It seems easier that way. As Adam and Eve hid from God because of their sin, so we all want to hide from God and hide our sin and hide from each other. That's the temptation. Why should a church not do that also and ignore sin?

In verses 6 to 8 we see that sin in the local church, if ignored, infects the whole church. 'Your boasting is not good. Do you not know that a little yeast works through the whole batch of dough?' (verse 6). Paul goes on to remind the Corinthians that in the Old Testament book of Exodus, God's people were rescued out of slavery in Egypt and they were told to bake some bread for the journey, unleavened bread that will be ready to eat more quickly. There is no need to put yeast in and wait for it to spread and have its effect through the dough. And the apostle Paul uses that image of yeast spreading through and impacting the whole loaf of bread.

We are like bread that should have yeast in us – good yeast. Verse 8 speaks of sincerity and truth, not bad yeast that has gone off, which is like malice and wickedness. If you put yeast in a loaf of bread it spreads through the whole loaf. It affects the whole loaf. If the yeast you put in the bread is rotten and off, the whole loaf will be rotten and off. But if the yeast you put in is good, then the whole loaf of bread will be edible and pleasant.

The illustration is simple. We are not living private lives, we are joined together by God's Spirit. The church is one loaf of bread, so to speak. And if there is one person who is ignoring God's will for their lives and fighting against Him and covering it up and people begin to become aware of it and they all ignore it; it is like yeast that spreads through the whole church family. Damage is done to everybody. We are not private individuals.

Our Church Mission Statement is 'Knowing God's Word, Building His People'. We build his people by adding to the church numerically, seeking to tell people about Jesus and inviting them to church, giving them the opportunity to find out about him. That is one way to build his church: numerically adding new people. We also build up his people by growing in maturity. We have begun to know God and are growing in our relationship with him, setting aside more and more sins, struggling to fight against them, helping each other to do that more. We build up by adding. We build up by spiritually growing in maturity. Both of those things go on.

We all find it really, really difficult to engage in trying to build up God's people numerically. Telling people who don't come to church, that we go to church, and inviting them to find out more. Telling somebody about what Jesus has done in my life. Sharing the story. We all find that difficult!

I wonder if we find it difficult because these two different ways of building up his Church are intimately linked together? That is, if we find it hard to help each other in the church family to deal with sin, to admit our struggles, to correct each other lovingly, if we find it really hard to build up His people in that biblical way inside the church family, well maybe it is not that surprising that we find it hard to build up God's people in the other way, by inviting other people to come in.

Perhaps building up God's people, reaching out and maturing the people that are here, are so intimately related to each other that as we begin to be more honest about our sins and help each other, correct one another more deeply, perhaps as we do that we will find ourselves growing in confidence and ability to ask other people to join us? It is possible that the Church was designed to work that way.

If then we ignore problems in one another's lives,

the yeast will spread and all of us will find that our relationships with one another and with God become corrupted.

The apostle Paul has great insight into human nature. He knows that we always find ways to misunderstand things! So he finishes off his argument in verses 9 to 13 by saying in effect, 'Look, you need to know the difference between sin in the world and sin in the church.' You know that stereotype of the church preaching against all the sin in the world out there. Like the man with the placard walking down the street telling all the people in the street that they have done all these terrible sins. And that is a stereotype of the church. We gather together in a building once a week to tell each other how bad all those people out there are. And it is possible to read this passage and begin to think like that. You know, it is really bad when people do x, y and z. We mustn't spend any time with those people out there. But Paul says, 'No. You must recognise the difference between sin in the church and sin in the world.' Verses 9 and 11 emphasise this.

'I have written to you in my letter not to associate with sexually immoral people, not at all meaning the people of this world who are immoral or greedy, swindlers, idolaters.' (verse 9).

'I am writing to you that you must not associate with anyone who calls themselves a brother but is sexually immoral, greedy an idolater or a slanderer, drunkard or swindler. With such a man do not even eat.' (verse 11).

The point is that people who do not know Jesus and do not trust in him, you should expect them to live in whatever way they want. We associate with them in the world and at work. We can become friends with them in all kinds of ways. We can enjoy sports together and get to know them and we do not need to sit in judgement of them. Paul is writing to a people who are involved in the church family, who profess Jesus Christ and live as if they do not have to obey God. That is the issue. We are not to become judgemental, looking down on people in the outside world. But we are to take very seriously what we believe. It should change how we live. And we need to help each other with that, within the church. We are not believing God's word if we ignore sin in the church.

What does that mean for our church? If we

ignored this kind of teaching in the Bible completely, then our relationships would begin to disintegrate. Christians who trust in Jesus and know the Bible would lose confidence in our church, and they would, rightly, not want to give money to support the ministry of our church because they would know that the church leadership do not take the Bible seriously. They would know that a church that ignored this kind of teaching just descends into chaos and falls apart. So a church trying to find ways to implement these teachings is a church which is taking God seriously. That you can trust. Sadly, in years gone by, it has been the case that when somebody is hurt or treated badly by someone in a church, when it is brought to the church minister's attention and others in the church, they tended to ignore it and cover it up. Perhaps the person who has been treated badly is themselves made to feel like it was their fault. That is appalling.

Having some kinds of systems and processes and safeguards in the church is necessary to reassure all of us that that will not happen in our church. What can we do? I will just mention a few little things. 95-97% of all this kind of discipline and care happens informally, privately in healthy relationships. In home groups, that's a key place. Do you love God enough to join a home group? Do you love other people in church enough to spend time with them that goes beyond sitting a few metres away from them in a pew? In a home group you have the opportunity to see people behave badly! And they have the opportunity to see you be greedy or gossipy or unkind. And if they love you enough and if you love them enough, they might, in an appropriate way, at the appropriate time, lovingly and gently try and help you. That would grow our church in wonderful ways.

When we look at employees of our church, we build into the contractual arrangement more than just a business exchange of money for services. We build into it an expectation of certain behaviours, of living out the Christian life – regular attendance at church, godly living and so forth. If that begins to change we have grounds and a framework to talk about it, to explore the reasons, and work out what the next best steps are. I myself as a minister, have a framework around me. If there are problems, people can come and talk to me, and if it is not resolved satisfactorily they can talk to other office holders and so forth.

Holy Communion is most important, is it not? It is the service when we gather as one church family to celebrate and enter more deeply into the benefits of the death of Jesus Christ. If it begins to become apparent that there is someone in church who is ignoring God's teaching for their lives and is not responding well to encouragement or challenge, then I would say to them, as I have done before, 'Look I really think you should refrain from taking Communion for a week or two. Go and talk to that person and say sorry to them and try to be reconciled. You will find that when you come back for Communion, God will bless you much more deeply.' Nobody even notices that it happens, but that is a process that has been helpful for numbers of people in churches, myself included.

If somebody insists on coming to Communion and refuses to accept any kind of correction or anything, well the words of the Book of Common Prayer which are read are a stern warning to us. 'Dearly beloved in the Lord ye that mind to come unto the Holy Communion of the body and blood of our saviour Christ must consider how St. Paul exhorts all persons diligently to try and examine themselves before they presume to eat of the bread and drink of that cup. For as the benefit is great, if with a true penitent heart and lively faith we receive that holy sacrament, so is the danger great if we receive the same unworthily, for then we are guilty of the body and blood of Christ our Saviour. We eat and drink our own damnation not considering the Lord's body. We kindle God's wrath against us. We provoke Him to plague us with diverse diseases and sundry kinds of death. Judge therefore yourselves brethren that ye be not judged.' Holy Communion then encourages us to help each other with our problems and sins.

All of the people who do ministry in our church in any formal capacity have to have signed Volunteer Agreements in which they promise to live out the basic expectations of people who are Christians and obey what God says in the Bible. I share that with you to reassure you that when you come forward for prayer in the side chapel after service, anybody who is permitted to exercise that ministry has signed an agreement like that. When you send your children out to Sunday Club, anybody who teaches there has signed an agreement like that. When you send your young teenager out to the youth group – the same is true. And it also applies to anybody who participates in music ministry at the front of church, or people who welcome at the door and so forth.

All this should reassure us that we take the Christian life seriously in our church, and if somebody begins to ignore what Jesus teaches in a flagrant way and will not respond to encouragement or challenge, then they will have to step back from volunteering or serving in a ministry. Anybody who does not accept that as part of the nature of ministry has not understood something very fundamental about the nature of the Christian life and ministry.

It is normal church life to have that kind of protection for all of us. Indeed every situation is unique and complicated. Still those are some of the very general safeguards we have. How we approach each individual has consequences for our whole church family. So let us try and take further steps to take our relationships with one another deeper and more seriously, because that is one of the ways we begin to take our relationship with God deeper and more seriously.

Don't be Fooled:
Change is Possible

1 Corinthians 6:9-20

THE CORINTHIAN CHURCH IN THE FIRST CENTURY was a little Christian community by a seaport, a place of trade and commerce where many different cultures met in a melting-pot of business, recreation and widely talked about immorality: to 'corinthianise' in the ancient world was a slang term for corrupting somebody morally. You can see the church in Corinth was indeed a tragic church as you read what was going on in the first and second letters to the Corinthians.

You discover a church which was riven apart by divisions. There were different groups in the church, each of which thought that they were better than the other and understood what God wanted better than the other. There was immorality which even people outside the church said was remarkable and spectacular in the damage it did to families and relationships. The people in the Corinthian church who were richer and better off than others in the church looked down on them, treated them badly and made them feel worse for their poverty.

And in the midst of all of this unpleasantness, the Corinthian church was remarkably proud. They thought they were spiritually superior to other Christians. As you read the letters of 1 and 2 Corinthians, a couple of big myths about church are exploded for us.

The first myth that many people believe today is that church is a place for perfect people who are really well-behaved. Well just read a few chapters of 1 and 2 Corinthians and you see that is clearly not the case because here is a church of people whose lives are a mess! When they got together Paul said in one part of Corinthians, 'Your meetings do more harm than good.' How would that feel as a verdict on your church? When you get together to have a church meeting or a church service, it would be better for you all to have stayed at home. You do that much damage to each other and to God's kingdom and to the reputation of God outside the church. It would be better if you all had stayed in bed and didn't bother turning up. That is the church of Corinth.

So, if you've come to church today and you feel, 'I have got problems, I have got struggles,' then you are welcome. Church is a place for people who can admit that. Church is not a place for perfect people. The Corinthian church was certainly not a church of people who were perfect or respectable.

Furthermore, as you see Paul writing to this church we see another myth exploded. Many today believe that deep substantial change is not really possible. The way I am today is the way I must stay. We read here of Paul bringing God's word to the troubled Corinthian church. In doing that Paul pastors them and teaches them and trains them. This led to people being changed. In many ways today our culture says, whatever you are, whatever lifestyle you have got, whatever burdens you have got, you are broadly speaking stuck with it for various reasons - your DNA, your family background, your education, your economic situation, all of these forces and powers are out of our control. They conspire together to say that whatever pattern of behaviour or struggle I have got, change is not going to be possible. Well, God doesn't accept that because when he writes to the Corinthian church through Paul's letters, he helps them see how God, bit by bit, can change people.

The Church of England has to decide whether it is going to mirror back to society the lifestyles society says are acceptable, or if it's going to say that God can change you and give you something even better than what you experience at present. We learn in First Corinthians that change is possible.

In 1 Corinthians 6:9-11 we hear God encouraging us to **embrace the fresh start Jesus offers.**

'Do you not know that the unrighteous will not inherit the kingdom of God? Do not be deceived: neither the sexually immoral, nor idolators, nor adulterers, nor men who practice homosexuality, nor thieves, nor the greedy, nor drunkards, nor revilers, nor swindlers will inherit the kingdom of God. And such were some of you.' (verses 9-11).

The kingdom of God is the place where God is in charge, where he is King, where he rules. Jesus proclaimed the kingdom of God in the Gospels. In the book of Acts, at the end and at the beginning of that book, you find it written that God was bringing his kingdom to earth. And here the apostle Paul talks about Christians as people who have come to live in God's kingdom. The fact that the phrase is used again and again throughout the New Testament is a reminder, by the way, that the apostle Paul taught the same things that Jesus taught. That old idea that Jesus had a different religious outlook to Paul really doesn't bear scrutiny when you read the New Testament.

Jesus brought God's kingdom to earth through His death and coming to life again. Paul explained to the churches what it really meant to live in God's kingdom: the change that it makes for us. It all fits together perfectly well; it is the same teaching. The kingdom of God makes a difference. The kingdom of God is different to the kingdoms of this world.

People like to think that all people are sort of in God's kingdom, all people are in God's family and coming to church just helps us along a little bit; a little bit of encouragement, a little bit of advice and counsel, a few more friends to help us get through.

No. When people come into God's kingdom, they are stepping out of the kingdom of this world and into a new kingdom, where they are radically changed and transformed. Have a look at verse 9: 'Do you not know that the unrighteous will not inherit the kingdom of God? Do not be deceived.' If we are to live in the kingdom of God, then God needs to change us from being wicked and being caught up in ways of living that do not please Him, to being people that are forgiven and changed. The kingdoms are different.

A very popular television drama at the moment is available on the Amazon online store. It is called 'The man in the High Castle.' It tells a story about the world today as if the Germans had won the Second World War. Hitler is still alive; he's a very old man. He is still presiding over an international empire. And when you look across at America where most of the story takes place, you find that the Eastern coast is ruled over by Germany and Hitler while the Western coast is ruled over by one of their great allies that helped them win World War Two: the Japanese. And in the middle are the Badlands, a sort of empty world of lawlessness and disorder and refugees. The Japanese kingdom is on the western coast and the German Empire on the eastern coast.

As the show moves between these two empires, you see two very different kingdoms, one of them shaped by the history of Germany, with its industrial mechanical prowess and all of the regalia of the Nazi empire taken to an exaggerated form. And then the Japanese empire on the other side of America, shaped by an ancient culture of Samurai warriors and the honour code and Japanese culture. Two very different kingdoms and when individual people manage to sneak across the Badlands from one kingdom to the other, it is very clear a massive change has happened in their expectations of safety, in the laws, in the culture, in the relationships. Well, in the same way, when someone becomes a Christian and they trust in Jesus, they step into God's kingdom, and it makes a radical difference to them. It changes all our relationships, dreams, attitudes and behaviours. It is no small thing to be brought out of this world's kingdom into God's kingdom.

Paul gives us a list of some of the behaviours and lifestyles that are perfectly normal and natural and comfortable in the kingdom of this world, but do not fit in God's kingdom. 'Do not be deceived: neither the sexually immoral, nor idolators, nor adulterers, nor men who practice homosexuality, nor thieves, nor the greedy, nor drunkards, nor revilers, nor swindlers will inherit the kingdom of God.'

It is helpful to read that list. I am sure it's not an exclusive, complete list. There are other lists in the New Testament that are slightly different, but it is helpful to see that there are some things there that we might because of our age or our culture or our background think, 'Oh yes, I know that's a big problem, a really troublesome lifestyle to God's kingdom.' But then there are other things where we might think, 'Surely that is not overly important.' But they are all thrown there into the list are they not? Which shows us they all matter to God. The things that we might think are small and unimportant matter to God. So, for example, we may not think that gossip or slander are that big a problem, but here they are mentioned in verse 10.

One of C S Lewis's books was called 'The Great Divorce.' It is an imaginary story where he pictures a group of people who are in hell, taking a bus ride as a day trip to visit heaven. They go to heaven and they wander around and they talk to the angels and talk to the people who have gone to heaven. Then they discover that they hate the idea of being in heaven; they cannot really enjoy it. It is an opportunity for C S Lewis to explore the nature of the small things, the small sins in this life that ultimately get magnified over a lifetime and lead to us no longer fitting in with God's kingdom.

Let me just read to you one of the conversations that Lewis pictures happening on this remarkable day trip: 'I am troubled because that unhappy creature doesn't seem to me to be the sort of soul that ought to be even in danger of damnation. She isn't wicked: she's only a silly, garrulous old woman who has got into a habit of grumbling, and one feels that a little kindness, and rest, and change would put her all right.' The woman he was referring to was a woman who had been a gossip, a moaner, a grumbler and the man thought that it seemed very unfair that she missed out on heaven. Her sins seemed to be quite small in comparison with so much of the evil in our world. But as he begins to explore more, he realises that from God's perspective what looked like a very small sin actually revealed a heart that was a long, long way from God. We so often conclude that behaviours and lifestyles are not that big a problem. That's why we need God to list and explain to us things that are, in fact, a barrier to being in God's kingdom.

When Paul talks about these behaviours and lifestyles, he says in verse 9, 'do not be deceived.' He has to say that because there will always be people who say these behaviours do not matter. At the moment, in the Church of England there is a lot of pressure to say that homosexual lifestyles are perfectly acceptable within God's kingdom, and so the Church should bless and celebrate them. It is because lots of people say that and because our culture reinforces that message, that we need to hear the warning 'Do not be deceived.' We can be deceived on this matter. We can come to wrong conclusions. And the thing about being deceived is that you do not think you are deceived – you are sure you are right. At the same time, we need to think of these other sins like greed, slander, gossip and not be deceived there either. They can just as easily keep us out of God's kingdom as those other matters. Every one of them matters and we must let God's word, not our desires or our culture, shape our thinking.

Jesus Christ offers a fresh start for us. When he offers us that fresh start, it doesn't necessarily change every aspect of our behaviour overnight. It does not immediately undo the consequences of a lifestyle in which we have lived for many years. We struggle; we fail in all kinds of ways. Still, becoming a believer does move us out of one kingdom into a new kingdom. Living under a new King, does make a real difference to us. Change is possible. The words of verse 11 are wonderfully encouraging to us: 'That is what some of you were. But you were washed, you were sanctified, you were justified.'

You were a gossip and you've been moved out of that kingdom into the kingdom of God. You were caught up in the homosexual lifestyle, but you have been changed. You were a thief, but you have been justified. God can change us and move us from one kingdom into another. We have no grounds whatsoever to look down on somebody else in our church family or to look down on somebody outside God's kingdom and think we are better than they are, because we are all in different ways caught up in these various struggles and behaviours. If we have, in any meaningful way, been released from any part of them, it is not because we have done anything in our own strength, it's because Jesus has begun to change us.

Verse 10 warns **do not be deceived.** 'Do you not know that the wicked will not inherit the kingdom of God? Do not be deceived.' This is why the Church must uphold the teaching about behaviours that God says are wrong and the genuine changes that Jesus can make in our lives. If we do not, we will prevent people coming into God's kingdom. It is that serious. If the Church begins to say that these behaviours do not really matter and we can begin to celebrate them or encourage them or bless them, then it will actually be stopping people enjoying the wonderful gift of coming into God's kingdom and having God change them: 'Do not be deceived.'

Change in the Christian life is of course difficult. It is a struggle to let God begin to change us. We live in God's kingdom but we still carry the burden of many aspects of our behaviours and so we need to be encouraged to embrace the motivations for change that God gives us in these passages. In verses 12 to 20 we are told to embrace certain motivations. These move us to flee these lifestyles and behaviours. While a number of issues are mentioned, there is a focus placed upon sexual immorality. The passage is concerned with sexual immorality in its many varied forms: any sexual activity outside of marriage between a man and a woman would be Paul's definition. That would include homosexuality which is mentioned, but it would also include living with someone you are not married to and being engaged in a sexual relationship. It would also include the hook-up culture at University. It would also include pornography, and an infinite variety of other things. In short, anything outside of marriage between a man and a woman - which God says he does bless and honour. I guess God focuses here on sexual immorality because it is so entangling. It is very damaging to us as individuals and to our relationships. All of us are designed as sexual creatures. We all have desires and longings, and these things manifest themselves in our hearts in different ways at different ages. It is part of the way we are made. Where our desires and behaviours fall short of God's standards, change is possible, when new motivations are embraced.

There are however those who say that it is not the teaching of Christianity that change is really possible

– that whatever one feels one's identity is, whatever one's behaviour pattern is – we have to just embrace it. But it is so basic to Christianity that God changes us that it is clearly taught in books for young children!

Have a look for example at this simple children's book on Christianity. It is called 'The Ology.' It's a little book for children 8 to 9 years old, and I was reading one of the chapters with one of my children last night about the way God changes us, and here in language designed for little children we have the teaching laid out for us that God can and does change us. The children's book tells us on page 171 that, 'God is always at work making us more and more like Jesus.' Yes there is a struggle, and yes we still sin. But children can understand the Bible's teaching that God changes us for the better.

Experiencing the power of this change requires that we know the motivations for change God gives us. We all need the motivations that God gives us in this passage to embrace the change of living in God's kingdom and to pick ourselves up again and continue when we fall. Let's look at the motivations for change God gives.

Motivation 1: God owns our bodies (verse 13).
The Corinthian church were trying to justify to Paul that it was acceptable for them to be involved in God's kingdom but at the same time to be involved in various kinds of sexual immorality. So they said, 'Everything is permissible for me' (verse 12). It was a catchphrase; a slogan. They explained it thus: 'Food for the stomach and the stomach for food.' That catchphrase or cliché in verse 13 seems to suggest they were thinking, 'My stomach is something I put food in, and that is all it does. It has nothing to do with anything more spiritual or more ethical, therefore I can do whatever I want with my body. I can continue a sexual relationship with somebody I am not married to or continue looking at that pornography. It is of no more interest to God than whether I have bacon or sausages for breakfast.' The Corinthians had these little clichés, these little phrases, to justify their behaviours.

There are similar slogans today, are there not? 'It's my body! I'm not hurting anyone! We're all consenting adults!' Lots of clichés and phrases that our culture uses to justify its behaviour. But Paul answers them and retorts: 'You say everything is permissible for me (verse 12), but you forget that not everything is beneficial.' Paul's answer is carefully argued: You say 'Everything is permissible for me,' but I reply, 'I will not be mastered by anything.' I am in God's kingdom. I want Him to be God over me. 'Food for the stomach, the stomach for food, but God will destroy them both. The body is not meant for sexual immorality, but for the Lord.' (verse 13) Paul is saying the Lord made our bodies. The Lord is in charge of us; he owns us. And therefore what we do with our bodies does matter. That is the first motivation - God owns our bodies.

Motivation 2: God will raise our bodies (verse 14). Later, in 1 Corinthians 15 Paul explores the reality and the implications of Jesus rising from the dead. It is a great misunderstanding of Christianity to think that it is merely a spiritual message or to think that it is merely lifestyle advice. No, it is a historical report about things that happened in history; that Jesus really did die on the cross, and he really did rise again from the dead, in his physical body. If you had been there you could have videoed it; you could have touched him with your hands. It was real. Jesus' real, physical, historical coming to life again is evidence that God will do the same for our bodies. The future of our bodies is caught up with and linked to the body of Jesus Christ. It means that what we do in our bodies today, has abiding significance. Our bodies are not for the rubbish heap – they will be renewed and taken on beyond the grave to a new creation.

Incidentally, this touches on a pastoral matter people quite often ask about. It might be helpful as an aside to address it. People sometimes ask me: Is there any difference from a Christian perspective about planning my funeral as a cremation or a burial? People wonder this and find it helpful to hear that the traditional answer is that in the ultimate sense it does not matter. God will raise all people to new life regardless of their means of funeral. And yet, it has also been thought that burial of people is more respectful of the body, because it is only in burial that human beings take no active steps to damage or destroy the physical body after death. But in cremation action is taken to destroy the body. It might be significant of course that while cremation was a form of funeral associated with pagan religions, it was not the way Christians in the early Church approached their funerals.

The first time Christians began to experience

cremation was when the Romans were persecuting them, and they heard that Christians believed their bodies would be raised again to new physical life. As a way of trying to mock them, and to say, 'Well, God won't be able to raise them after cremation!' They began to burn the bodies of Christians. Now, of course, in the ultimate sense, God can raise our bodies even if we have been cremated. But it is a pastoral implication of the fact that our bodies really do matter, that burial is often preferred by Christians. From the perspective of this passage, the key application is of course, that our behaviour in this life matters because it is done in bodies which will be raised to new life by Jesus.

Motivation 3: The Spirit lives in us (verse 18). The temple in the Old Testament was the place where God lived; a place where God's people could come to his presence. So there was a time when God wanted his presence to be identified in a special way with a building – the temple. But people are very wrong if they think that the church building we are in today is the place where God lives for us! This is a beautiful building, 150 years old – a splendid specimen of Victorian architecture. But from a spiritual perspective it is nothing more than a rain shelter- a rain shelter which leaks quite a bit sadly. It is just a building. The temple, the place where God lives, is in the body, the heart, the lives of anybody who has come into His kingdom by trusting in Jesus. This means that as we continue to explore with other churches in Tunbridge Wells over the next few years, establishing new little congregations, new worshipping communities where people can find out about Jesus, we are liberated from the false idea that we need a building like this. Christians can meet anywhere because the temple is anyone's body in which God's Spirit comes to live. And of course that means that what we do with our bodies matters. The Spirit lives in us. He begins to change us from the inside out. It's a great motivation to pick ourselves up again if we've failed, and embrace further change.

Motivation 4: Jesus bought us (verse 20). Finally, and particularly helpful for us as we come forward to Communion, a motivation to resist immorality in our bodies is that Jesus bought us. 'You were bought with a price.' When Jesus died on the cross, he paid a price to purchase us for God's kingdom, therefore we belong to him, and He cares about what we do. I have two cars sitting in my driveway at the moment. If one of them gets scratched and damaged, I will be very upset. If the other one gets scratched and damaged, I will not mind so much! One of the cars belongs to me. I paid for it. The other one belongs to a friend from church – I am just looking after it for them while he is on holiday. If I am honest, between you and me, I care more about my car than his, because I bought it, I paid for it! When God looks down upon his world, he sees people who are in his kingdom. Jesus died for them. He paid a price to buy them for himself and therefore he really cares about what we do with his purchase – our bodies and lives.

Let us prayerfully ask God to take these motivations for change and to plant them deeper in our hearts so that we can be ready to fight afresh, to live in God's kingdom and embrace the change he gives us.

Contend for the Faith

The Letter of Jude

THE LETTER OF JUDE is a short one-chapter book written by 'Jude, a servant—or a slave, actually—of Jesus Christ, and a brother of James.' (verse 1) The James referred to is the same person who wrote the letter of James in the New Testament. He was a brother of Jesus, which, if my family tree is correct, would make Jude a brother of Jesus also. James the brother of Jesus and Jude the brother of Jesus.

Earlier on in his life, Jude would have been one of the family members who went along to Jesus while he was in a house teaching people about the kingdom of God, and told onlookers that Jesus was mad – out of his mind! (Mark 3:31-34) 'Come home! Stop embarrassing yourself Jesus,' Jude would have said.

And I guess, as the years went on, Jude must have changed his mind and realised that Jesus was in fact God himself. Jude would no longer refer to himself as a 'brother' of Jesus – one who would tell him what to do, as if he was in charge and he knew better. No, he prefers to be known as a 'slave' of Jesus. He doesn't even mention the biological relationship to Jesus: 'I will respectfully refer to myself as simply a brother of James.'

There is something quite beautiful about the humility of no longer bossing Jesus around, and not saying any more, 'I know what is right, you should say what I want you to say.' Now Jude has become the kind of person who allows God to tell him, 'You are wrong in your desires and thinking. I am right; change your views.'

So Jude writes a letter to the churches, a very short letter. It is a letter all about arguing and fighting and contending for the Christian message. And lots of people would say – and we feel it ourselves do we not – that contending and arguing for the Christian faith is a bit of a distraction from the real job of ministry. It is something that maybe some people might do if they have the right personality or position of influence, but generally speaking it is a distraction or it is optional.

Jude argues that it is not a distraction and it is not optional. 'Dear friends, although I was very eager to write to you about the salvation we share, I felt I had to write and urge you to contend for the faith that was once for all entrusted to the saints.' (Jude 3,4)

Jude had wanted to write about all the kinds of stuff we would normally expect ministers to be talking about. You know, I wanted to write to you about the plans for that building project, I wanted to write to you about the plans to train new Sunday school teachers, I wanted to write to you about the next sermon series, or the next social event we have where you can bring your friends to hear about Jesus. All the things you would expect the church to want to talk about, Jude says, 'I wanted to do them, but there was something more important. I had to set all of that aside, and instead, I felt I had to write and urge you to contend for the 'Faith' that was once for all entrusted to you.'

We think of the word 'faith' as meaning our trust in God, and that is what it often means in the Bible, but it also can be used in more of a capital 'F' way. The Faith: the body of truths revealed in Scripture about God which you have to hold to in order to have access to the real Jesus. Holding to the correct 'Faith' is the only way to put your 'faith' in the genuine Jesus.

The Faith is not something that can be changed. Lots of people today say that the Faith evolves and changes with the culture. God reveals himself through the culture around us, and as the culture changes, the Faith changes to keep up with it. And therefore, in those cultures in the world different to our own, the Faith would be different to here. Not so. In the Bible, the Faith was 'once for all entrusted', which is such a very strong phrase. The Faith was given; it is the shape it is and it can never be changed. The Faith.

Jude said, I had to write and urge you to contend for that unchangeable, given body of claims and truths revealed by God to his people. Defending the Faith is not a distraction from ministry; it is vitally important. Jude puts it at the top of his agenda because people in the church have begun to say things that contradict, undermine, and push away the real Faith.

It may be tempting to say when you are making a lovely cake for your grandmother, 'Oh, I accidentally knocked over a small bottle of poison, and a few drops of it fell into the cake mix. But it is alright: it is only a couple of drops, I did not pour it all over the cake liberally! I will just bake it up, put some icing on, make it look good and I will feed it to her anyway.' No, a tiny little bit of poison spreads through the whole cake. It is serious. If you have spilt poison on the cake mix, you cannot ignore it, you cannot get on with the icing and choose which candles to put on top - you need to deal with the poison.

So it is in the church also. 'Certain men whose condemnation was written about long ago have secretly slipped in among you. They are godless men, who change the grace of our God into a license for immorality and deny Jesus Christ our only Sovereign and Lord.' (Jude 4).

They have sneaked into the church; therefore they are deceptive. They do not walk around carrying a big placard saying, 'Hello, I am a false teacher, I am here to deceive you.' No, they sneak in. They probably look far more credible as church ministers than I do. You do not spot them by the way they walk or their clothing. There are so many ways people can deny the faith, but Jude highlights one of the most important and most common; this has been a huge challenge for the Church down the years: 'They change the grace of our God into a license for immorality.' (verse 4). By doing so they deny that Jesus really is Lord.

The grace of God is the most powerful and moving and wonderful part of the Christian message. It is the claim that God does not treat us as we deserve. That we all mess up, that we all sin, that we all do things that make him angry, but he does not pour out his anger upon us; he doesn't beat us up. He creates a way, through the death of Jesus, to forgive us. He gives us the undeserved gift of a relationship with him – forgiveness now, heaven for ever. And we do not deserve it, neither do we earn it: it is a gift of grace. Grace means something that I did not do anything to deserve; it is a free gift.

It is very easy for people to take the Christian message of grace, and then begin to reason and argue, 'Because God does not give me what I deserve, because he gives me heaven and forgiveness by grace, on the basis of what Jesus did and not what I did, therefore it does not really matter how I live, or what I do. I can use his grace as an excuse to ignore something that God has said in the Bible.'

Pastorally it can become complicated. It is possible for two people to look like they are both ignoring what God says in the Bible, but one of them may be flagrantly and proudly using God's grace as an excuse to shake their fist at God, and do what they want in their life. The other person may have a life that looks very similar, but actually the person has fallen into sin, they are greatly pained by it, they try their best to recover, and they trust Jesus and resolve to repent. It may look similar for a season, but the second person is not shaking their fist at God and fighting him. They are depending on his grace and slowly God is working in their heart and he will one day take them to heaven — by grace. You do not always know what goes on in somebody's heart. We must admit and be sensitive to that.

But of course what Jude is talking about is rather

different. He writes of the people in the church who teach certain things. When you look at the words they've written down, or the messages they have given to their congregations, or the votes they have passed, they in effect say to the church, 'Because God is gracious, it does not matter how you live. It may appear that God wants that area of your life to be changed but since God is full of grace, he will overlook it and accept you as you are.' The false teachers change the grace of God into a license for immorality.

And Jude says, when that goes on, it is really serious. You cannot ignore it. You put it to the top of the agenda and you must deal with it. This is one of the main points that Jude makes through the whole argument of his letter and it's a really obvious insight. It's not a really complicated idea that requires great theological insight and years of training to grasp. False teachers always hurt God's people and so they must be contended against.

This is foundational to God's revelation in the past, in the Old Testament. So many of the stories of the Old Testament show people in Israel fighting against what God says, and in doing so, great damage to God's people is caused. They had to be dealt with.

The New Testament teaches it as well; in fact Jude even quotes (twice) from books that are not in the Bible at all, just general popular religious books of the day. That suggests that even the average person who does not know what the Bible says apart from a vague recollection of Sunday school or a passing reference to a rather second-rate book on religion knows that false teachers are trouble. Even such an uninformed person would know that when you have a message from God that changes your life by giving you a new relationship with God and saving you from hell for heaven and then someone comes along teaching something different, it is a really serious problem that must be dealt with.

Jude says, 'Though you already know all this,' (verse 5) and then he mentions several Old Testament stories. After that he says, 'Dear friends, remember what the apostles of our Lord Jesus told us.' (verse 17). The apostles were the authoritative New Testament teachers.

So Jude's reasoning is that you already know, if you know anything about the Bible in the Old or New Testaments, or even about religion in general, you know dealing with false teachers is vital.

Let me draw your attention to a couple of the examples in the Old Testament. 'I want to remind you that the Lord delivered his people out of Egypt, but later destroyed those who did not believe.' (verse 5). You can imagine the false teacher. They will look credible.

In our context, whatever you imagine a Church of England minister should be like, that will be what they will look like. And they will be saying, 'Look, God is a God of grace, God is a God of love. Once he has saved you, if you ignore something he says and you sin, it does not matter, remember he is a God of grace. Once saved, always saved. God loves you, he will never let you go.'

Jude replies, did you ever read the book of Exodus? Exodus chapter 32, in particular. God has saved his people from Egypt. It is the great picture of the rescue that Jesus gives his people in the New Testament. After they have been saved, one of the leaders of God's people, Aaron, taught the people that they could worship other gods. They engaged in immorality together in a very public way. Moses came back down the mountain and he was angry and he did what God told him to do.

Moses said to them, 'This is what the Lord, the God of Israel, says: 'Each man strap a sword to your side. Go back and forth through the camp of Israel from one end to the other, each killing his brother and friend and neighbour.' The Levites did as Moses commanded, and that day about three thousand of the people died.' (Exodus 32:27).

That was how God told Moses to deal with God's people when they followed the false teachers. It is a horrific picture. It is obviously not what we are supposed to do today; we are in a different situation. Yet it shows that God does not tolerate false teaching.

Jude points out that if your understanding of Christianity is merely that God is a God of love and a God of grace so it does not matter what you do – remember Exodus. Many other stories in the Old Testament are mentioned here showing the same thing.

In the New Testament, the apostles did likewise. 'They said to you, 'In the last times there will be scoffers who will follow their own ungodly desires.' These are the men who divide you.' (verse 18).

People say that the church leaders who point out false teaching are divisive. 'Keep quiet! Be more positive, tow the party line, wait and see how things work out. You're being negative and divisive.' But Jude says, 'No, no, no! The divisive person is the person who introduces into God's Church teachings that pull people away from God. They are the ones who are dividing God's people. It was not Moses' fault that Aaron did what he did in Exodus. Moses was not the divisive one.'

I think that as the book of Jude suggests, we know that this is the case. We know in our hearts that Christianity is a message which is wonderful and life-giving, and when people come along and try to change it, that does great damage to God's people.

We have to find ways to contend for the Faith. We need to be prepared for that. It is not easy. And so you would think Jude would argue in his book that you should run away as fast as you can from any false teachers – do not get anywhere near them – ignore them and just focus on reading the Bible for yourself and being involved in your local church.

And yet in a counter-intuitive way, in order to

help people to know what they should do when the time comes, Jude says we must get to know false teachers better! Get to know false teachers better? He does not mean by going along and joining their church, listening to their teaching and enjoying sitting under it. He says get to know false teachers better by reading your Bible more carefully, spending more time meditating on the pictures in the Old Testament and the New Testament of what God says false teachers are really like. You need to do this because they are sneaky, they are deceptive, you will not recognise them just by what they wear and how they look or their accent!

If you meditate on the Bible's pictures of the people who tried to lead God's people astray in the past, you will know false teachers with a depth of understanding and spiritual insight that they do not even have of themselves. They presume to tell God's people what to do, they claim to be in charge, they claim to know God's will for people's lives, but Jude says, they are like clouds that just drift around blown by the wind, they are like autumn trees without fruit and uprooted. They do not understand what they do; they are like instinctive, unreasoning animals. (verse 10). These are Jude's descriptions, and if you meditate on the Bible you will understand false teachers better than they understand themselves. You will recognise them when they come along.

Let me draw your attention to an important verse. This will help you recognise false teachers in the Church against whom we must contend. 'Woe to them! They have taken the way of Cain; they have rushed for profit into Balaam's error; they have been destroyed in Korah's rebellion.' (verse 11). Those three Old Testament people are characters to ponder and meditate on.

Cain, in Genesis 4, murdered his brother. His brother was a member of God's people. You do not get greater hatred for God's people than actually killing one of them. Why did he do it? Read Genesis 4 and you will find that Cain and Abel were both religious men, and both worshipped God, they were both members of God's people. But God looked at the offering that each man brought, and God received and welcomed the worshipful offering Abel brought. He did not commend the offering that Cain brought. We do not know why. Now Cain was enraged at that, and it led to him killing his brother. What motivated Cain? What did he long for and lust after so much that he would murder a member of God's people – his own brother?

He longed for religious acceptance and status. And so, it is not surprising what betrayals, what manipulations, what broken friendships men will inflict upon others that they are close to, in order to have some kind of religious status in the church. Somebody who just wants to be in charge of the home group. Somebody who just wants to make sure that they are nominated to be the bishop ahead of another person. It is astonishing what men will do for religious status and acceptance. It began in Genesis 4 and it leads people today to say things in the Church that are wrong. If joining the club of religious acceptance requires you teach something false, many will happily do it even if it hurts believers.

In Numbers 22 we read about Balaam, the man who was corrected by his donkey. It is an astonishing story. Balaam was a prophet in God's people and Balak was a king. He looked out at God's people and said, 'There are too many of them! They are going to overrun the country! I cannot get these people to pay taxes. My own people are going to be in danger of this great growing nation.' So he sends some messengers to deploy a tactic still used today. The false teacher makes an offer through intermediaries. The intermediaries come to Balaam the prophet, and they say to him, 'Would you please give us a sermon in which you tell God's people that God is cursing them, even though he said through Abraham that he was going to bless them? You know, give a message that will put God's people down; say the opposite of what God says.' And Balaam tries to do it. You can read the story for yourself and find that God overruled it.

But the point for Jude is Balaam tried again and again to preach against God's people. Balaam was tempted and gave in. Why? Very simple, the age-old temptation: cold, hard cash. As Judas betrayed Jesus for silver, Balaam betrayed his office as a teacher to God's people for money. It has seduced many people. I have on one occasion been offered an envelope full of £100 notes in order to conduct an illegal wedding. I jokingly checked with my boss if we could use it for the building project before declining the money. That was a crass attempt at bribery. Of course, the offer usually comes much more subtly.

It could be a matter of hoping you are on the right committee to make sure that the renovations to the vicarage will be done for you and not that other person. It is just keeping quiet because you know that somebody is a major giver to your church and they really do not like that part of the Christian message. If you mention it, they might stop giving. It is just that willingness to hold back from a costly course of action because it might make you a little uncomfortable, or maybe it will make you most uncomfortable. It will affect the schooling of your children, your holiday plans. All of these things seduce the teachers of God's people such that they are willing to not contend against the false teachers and perhaps eventually become one themselves.

A final example is Korah. We read his story in Numbers 16. Moses was leader of God's people and Korah and some of his friends and family got together to hold a public meeting with Moses. We need to have a public discussion, an open meeting – it is a very civilised way of doing business! And at this meeting, Korah said to Moses, 'You have led God's people out of slavery in Egypt, God has spoken through you, you are the leader of God's people – but why should you be in charge now? I want to be in charge. My family should have a more authoritative role in the running of God's people.' And God's response was to have Korah killed. You can read the story for yourself: stern, serious and scary.

Cain was motivated by a lust for religious acceptance and prestige; Balaam was motivated by a lust for money and comfort; Korah was motivated by a lust for authority and power. If you keep those pictures in front of you, if you meditate on them, you will know false teachers in the Church better than they know themselves. You will recognise them when they come along, and you will know how to contend.

It seems frightening to think that within God's Church we are not really safe. There are people who will lead us astray and they will hurt people. But we do not need to fear, we do not need to worry, because Jude finishes with a wonderful, positive, confidence-giving message: God will keep his people. He opens his letter by saying it: 'To those who are loved by God and kept by Jesus Christ' (verse 1). So we are kept by Jesus. And also at the very end of the letter, 'To him who is able to keep you from falling.' (verse 24).

So though we are weak, though we do not know everything in the Bible and are all still learning, though the false teachers are clever, deceptive and motivated by overwhelming lusts for things they want – despite all that, we are kept and we will be kept. God will look after us and get us through.

But we do have a duty and responsibility. In the middle of all that reassurance, in the middle of being told that God will keep us, we are taught, 'Dear friends, build yourselves up in the most holy Faith and pray in the Holy Spirit. Keep yourselves in God's love.' (verse 20).

Yes you are kept, but you must keep yourself. If you wilfully ignore the bits of the Bible that do not fit with what you think God should say, then you are in great danger. You are not building yourself up in the holy Faith, rather you are trying to force God into saying what you want him to say. Let God be God! Let God say what he wants! He is God! We can be wrong; he corrects us.

When we listen to what God says in the Faith, we find that we are being kept and we keep ourselves in God's love. We are able to wait for Jesus to come back to complete his work. We have to work to build ourselves up and keep ourselves: in a home group, in private reading of the Bible, in regular coming to church, in a hunger to grow in our understanding. As we engage in these efforts, God uses them to keep us. Let me finish with that final great prayer from Jude:

'To him who is able to keep you from falling and to present you before his glorious presence without fault and with great joy—to the only God our Saviour be glory, majesty, power and authority, through Jesus Christ our Lord, before all ages, now and for evermore! Amen.'

Is Love Really All You Need?

The Second Letter of John

IN 1967 THE BEATLES released their famous song 'All you need is Love' and in many ways it set the tone and the agenda for not only the 1960s, but the subsequent decades: all you need is love.

Love would be placed as the top priority for many people's lives. But we get confused about what love is. So if I want to marry a person, love shapes that decision . . . but love also shapes the decision of leaving that person for somebody else. Love is an empty vessel into which is poured whatever it is that I feel I want. Whatever I feel I need from you or the world around me, well that is love to me. If you do not let me do or be what I want to do or be, then you are lacking love to me. All you need is love – it is all important but undefined.

Love has become a 'hooray' word; a word that as soon as it is mentioned in any context whatsoever, meaning whatever anybody wants it to mean, people cheer and say 'hooray'. It is love, it must be good, we must support whatever is being spoken of. It becomes a knock-down argument in the culture. Then this culture began to shape the Church. People began to expect the Christian church to behave in exactly the same way as the world.

If you love me you will let me do or be whatever I want. After all John the disciple of Jesus in his previous letter made one of his most famous comments about God, 'God is Love' (1 John 4:8). You can see how easily the culture's empty vessel of the word 'love' began to control agendas in the Church as well as the culture. 'God is love,' therefore whatever it is I want from my life, the Church must support it and validate it. God would want me to have this or to be this because God is love.

One way to test the reasonableness of all this is to read all of the letters written by John. The apostle

John was one of the disciples of Jesus. He wrote John's gospel and also three short letters 1, 2 and 3 John. If anybody knew about love and what loving relationships really are, it surely was John.

He was described as the 'beloved disciple' of Jesus. Jesus doubtless cared for and loved all of his disciples, but it seems there was something about John that meant he was a man who particularly attracted and engendered meaningful, deep, substantive loving relationships. He was part of the inner circle of the disciples of Jesus. And so throughout John's Gospel and indeed his three letters the theme of love rises right to the top of the agenda.

If you asked me to find a bit of the Bible which focuses on love, I would surely turn to something written by the apostle John. 'God is love' as he said in 1 John 4:8. You can see something of the depth of his relationships in the final comment of this little letter, 'I have much to write to you but I do not want to use paper and ink, instead I hope to visit you and talk with you face to face so that our joy may be complete.' (2 John 12). Is it not a delightful comment? You can see the depth of concern and love. The aged disciple John really wants to go and see the people he is writing to. Paper and ink are not enough. Real love demands a visit in person.

John is writing to those described as the 'chosen lady and her children'. (2 John 1) It may be a woman like Lydia in the book of Acts, a wealthy business woman who became a disciple of Jesus. After her heart was opened to God she opened up her home and used her large estate as a place where her little church family could meet to worship.

It may well be that this is the kind of situation we have here. The elder, John the disciple of Jesus, writing to a lady who is using her resources to support a little church family. 'To the chosen lady and her children whom I love' (verse 1). This relationship – this love – is a major theme of the letter. If John is somebody who knew that God is love, if John is somebody who loves this lady and the church that meets around her and if John is indeed the beloved disciple of Jesus, are the Beatles correct? Is it really the case that 'all you need is love'? Are we correct to think that love is an empty vessel into which we can pour whatever we think we want or need and it will be validated by God and his Church? All you need is love?

If you read on in this second letter of John you will find it is a bit more complicated. In verses 1-6 of the letter we see that **love needs truth**.

Now if love is a 'hooray' word for our culture, truth is the opposite; truth is a 'boo, hiss' word! When people talk about the need for truth, that sounds very negative, so sterile, so restrictive, so one-sided. Postmodern academics have spent many years arguing that there is not really any such thing as objective truth, there are just different opinions, varied subjective viewpoints. It can be summed up in the title which the band The Manic Street Preachers chose for one of their albums: 'This is my truth, tell me yours'.

Truth in the Bible is not sterile, nor negative, nor restrictive. Truth is essential. Jesus himself said: 'I am the way, the truth and the life'. (John 14:6). When John writes this little letter to a lady and the church around her, he talks about love, but note also the use of the word 'truth' in verse 1: 'To the chosen lady and her children, whom I love in the truth—and not I only, but also all who know the truth—because of the truth, which lives in us and will be with us for ever.'

The love that John has for this lady is shaped by and constrained by the truth. The truth is not sterile nor unrelational, the truth lives in him and is what animates his love and very life.

Something shapes all of our lives. There is something that animates us, that gets us excited, that leads us to prioritise a thing with our money, time and our energy, as opposed to something else. For a serious athlete, it is the time given to the training, to dieting in a particular way. For the entrepreneur it is getting the project to be successful. They will re-mortgage their house, they will resign from their job, they will focus all of their spending and energies upon making their product a success. What is it for you? What is it that shapes your life? The thing that you care about more than anything else?

For many it may be children, for many it may be the retirement dream, for many it will be something to do with work or a career. We all have something that shapes and constrains our life. The apostle John suggests the thing that should shape and constrain our life is the truth. This truth is Jesus and everything that is necessary to give us access to Him. When the truth is the frame of our life, then we are able to love other people and God in the way

God wants us to; in the way that is true to reality as God designed it.

The notion that a life shaped by love can mean whatever I want it to mean quite simply does not work. 'It has given me great joy to find some of your children walking in the truth just as the Father commanded us.' (verse 4). 'Walking' is one of those great Bible words that is used to sum up the idea of a life. Life is a walk, a journey, a pilgrimage. As we journey we are pilgrims through this world. John says it gives him great joy and happiness and pleasure to know that these children (these Christians) are walking in the truth. Our lives are to be shaped by the truth about Jesus and God.

Verse 5 then places a great priority upon the Christian believer's life, to consist of love to one another, 'Now dear lady I am not writing you a new command but one we have had from the beginning, I ask that we love one another.' Verse 4 and verse 5 are not contradictory. The apostle John did not just have a mental flip as he wrote verse 4 and accidentally followed it with something that is totally different and totally contradictory. They fit together perfectly; you can't have one without the other. To walk in the truth and to love one another: they are an organic whole. Love needs truth. Truth needs love. Our culture is very, very wrong and does great damage in its pulling apart of truth and love, suggesting you can just love people with no real understanding of the truth of what God says about the situation. It is not loving to let people keep thinking they can view anything at all as loving. Love needs truth.

This means that if I am trying to live my life as best I can and I do not know what the Bible says about Jesus, I do not know what God says is right or wrong in his world, then my failure to have access to that truth makes it impossible for me to love God or to love other people. I may use the word, 'love,' but it is just a vessel into which I have poured alien ideas and understandings. Real love needs truth.

The incredible good news of Christianity is that we are not left to wander through this world making up our own truth or to argue with other people about what truth is, with no way to resolve the debate. God has stepped into this world in the person of Jesus Christ. I know that many of you have discovered that for yourselves – God has stepped into this world just as John said at the start of his gospel. The Word has become flesh and made His dwelling among us. God came into this world as Jesus Christ. In Jesus, God has revealed to the world what God is really like, what he cares about, what is right, what is wrong and what He will do to fix our lives and fix our world. We are liberated to hold on to that truth. We are empowered to love God and love others, just as God designed. It all hinges upon God coming into this world as Jesus, in a real historical sense. He left his marks and his evidence through history and in his words and his teachings in the Bible. Through all this we have access to the real Jesus. See how important it is for God to become a human being and then to leave the record of what he said and did for us; through this we have access to the truth, so that we can love God and love one another rightly.

If I was following some other religion like Buddhism for example, I could take a book which summarises the teachings of Buddha and I could do what it says. I have a friend who used to be a Buddhist monk and he has gone into considerable detail with me about what it meant for his life to fully embrace the teachings of Buddhism. He says that without a doubt, following the teachings of

Buddhism will make you a lot more peaceful and content; it will change your life if you do everything that it says. Get up early enough, focus your breathing, do the exercises, tell yourself that what it says about reincarnation is right. It will change your life and broadly speaking, it may well do so for the better.

But the teachings of Buddhism differ from the teachings of Christianity, in a most important way. If by the wave of a magic wand, I could change the past such that Buddha never existed, he just vanished out of the historical records of the world, but I kept a copy of the book that records his teachings, I could just as well follow those teachings and they would have quite precisely the same impact on my life as if Buddha had existed. His real historical existence has no impact whatsoever upon the power of that book to change my life. That is the difference between religious advice and historical record.

The truth of Buddha's existence is entirely discontinuous with the impact of his teachings. With Jesus it is totally different. Our connection to Jesus and the power he brings into our lives to love God and love one another is absolutely dependent upon him really existing. If God did not become a human being in Jesus, then all of his teachings are a lie. In fact, if the whole thing is made up, then his teachings are a deception and will bring great disappointment, hurt and suffering into the life of anyone who tries to follow them. We should feel really, really sorry for Christians if Jesus Christ was not the God who become a human being.

This really matters. There is a huge, strong link between the truth of Jesus being God, what he said, and his impact on the lives of anybody that follows his teaching. You cannot separate what God did in Jesus from the teachings left behind in the Bible about him. Therefore Christianity has a huge concern about guarding and upholding the truth of the teachings in the Bible. If they are neglected, destroyed, or shut away, then we will have no access to Jesus, the Truth, who brings God's love into our hearts. We need to guard and uphold the teachings of Scripture, or else we stop people experiencing the love of Jesus for themselves.

So John, the most loving of Jesus' disciples, who wrote passionately about a God of love and longed to see the Christians grow in their love for one another, also warns the Christian church that there are many people who twist and hide and distort the teaching about Jesus. 'Many deceivers who do not acknowledge Jesus Christ as coming in the flesh have gone out into the world, any such person is a deceiver and the antichrist.' (verse 7).

In popular culture, we think of an antichrist as being a great monstrous being at the end of time. Now there is some indication in the Bible that there will be some great leader who sums up all of the rage and hatred towards Jesus, before Jesus finally returns to his world. But also in the writings of John and through the Bible we find the idea that anybody who takes a committed stand against the teachings of Jesus is in some ways a mini-antichrist. There are many such people in the world who stand against the truth of Jesus; many 'deceivers' as John calls them in verse 7.

They do not acknowledge that Jesus has come in the flesh. By implication they do not view Jesus' teachings as authoritative. They do not believe that a human man can in fact be God in flesh; uniquely authorised to reveal God's words. They do not view the teachings of Jesus' apostles as being held in the high regard that Jesus said they ought to be. They argue against core teachings of Jesus Christ and the

Christian faith. And since John loves the church, because he wants people to really love one another, he warns them about the deceivers. Their stand against the authority of Jesus is an attack on the Church's ability to love God and one another. Their 'love' is not in 'truth.'

It is a bit scary and uncomfortable to say that we are in danger while in church. We like to think of church as a place of safety and security in our relationships with one another. But the Bible repeatedly warns us that we are in danger of deception – while in church. The difficulty about being deceived is you do not know that you have been deceived. That is the nature of deception.

The people who come along with ideas and teachings that do not fit with the teachings of Jesus, will not carry a placard that announces 'I am a deceiver!' Quite the opposite - they will look like really credible leaders of God's church. However you imagine a minister, or a bishop or a church leader or a religious commentator should appear, that is how the deceptive leader will look.

The apostle John urges all Christians: Watch yourselves. 'Watch out you do not lose what you have worked for, but that you may be rewarded fully.' (verse 8). We do indeed need to watch out; we need to take a real interest in and concern about our own understanding of what God says in the Bible. The deceptions are very subtle: 'Anyone who runs ahead and does not continue in the teaching of Christ does not have God, whoever continues in the teaching has both the Father and the Son.' (verse 9). This verse suggests that the deceivers to watch out for are people who at one stage in life held to Jesus' teaching unashamedly and with great clarity. Perhaps they did so for decades, but now they merely acknowledge it as a 'formational part of my spiritual journey'; they insist they have since come to 'learn from the culture' this or that new insight. They deceive, saying, 'I am not rejecting my past, of course it was a wonderful work of God in my life, I just have to be open to what God is doing in this new situation.' That is the sort of language that is used. It is very subtle; they have built up years of trust and credibility and now they are just beginning to go a little bit further, to explore something new, seeking a new way to approach our relationships with one another or God and His church.

We have to watch out, we need to know what the

Bible really says for ourselves. As a minister I can teach you the best I can. I can direct you to books about the Bible, to help you understand the Bible better. But in the end, every individual is responsible for their own soul. We must all watch out for ourselves. None of us can know everything, none of us can learn everything in the Bible overnight. The full extent of God's revelation cannot be injected into us instantly, but we can all take a few more steps, can we not? We can read a few more pages in the morning, think about it, pray about it, ask a friend in church what it means, ask for a recommendation of another book. We could all join a home group to continue to read the Bible together with some people in church. Watch yourselves. Deceivers are effective and they do deceive many.

Secondly, John says to the church, as you begin to work out who these deceivers are and what they are saying, 'Do not welcome them.' (verses 10-11). Again, we like to think of church as a place that is welcoming and I hope that it is! I hope you received a warm welcome to church when you came in the door. I hope that it goes deeper; that people continue to talk with one another after the formal bit of the service and have coffee and refreshments afterwards. I hope that phone numbers and emails are exchanged and friendships develop during the week. Let us be a welcoming church!

But if we are going to be a loving and faithful church, we will not welcome everyone. 'If anyone comes to you and does not bring this teaching, do not take him into your house, or welcome him, anyone who welcomes him shares in his wicked work.' (verse 10). Strong words here insisting there are people the Church must not welcome. Anyone who runs on ahead of the teachings of Jesus thereby deceives people, leading them away from the love of God and the truth of God. Such a person should not be welcomed.

This means that if we fund, resource, support, commend, or have fellowship with a church leader, who upon careful examination looks like they are falling into John's category of being a deceiver, then we are as bad as they are. 'Anyone who welcomes him, shares in his wicked work.' (verse 10). Such strong words, but these are not my words; they are God's words recorded in the Bible.

The popular idea that unity and welcoming one another are to be at the top of the church's agenda is simply not correct. We are not to provide support to or have fellowship with people who run ahead of Jesus' teachings. Unity with them and welcoming them is not godly – it is rebellious. Ironically those who commend fellowship with false teachers are themselves running ahead of Jesus' teaching.

In our Book of Common Prayer service of Holy Communion, we pray for the unity of the wider Church. This is not unity at any cost. The words written by Cranmer were very carefully phrased, 'Grant that all they who do confess Thy holy name, may agree in the truth of Thy holy Word and live in unity and Godly love.'

When the churches agree in the truth of God's word, then those churches can enjoy unity. That unity is only possible under God's truth. Only when they live out a shared commitment to all God says can they really love one another and love a broken world.

Mission cannot be built upon contradictory views of Jesus' teachings. That is exactly the teaching of 2 John and indeed the rest of the Bible. This means that when a church holds to the truth of God's word, they are not being difficult, divisive, narrow minded or awkward. They are not being arrogant, nor are they breaking the unity of the Church. A church which seeks to uphold the teaching of God's word, the truth of Scripture, is being loving and faithful. They are seeking the only kind of unity that God blesses.

The apostle John delights to hear that churches are loving one another. The only way we can develop loving churches is by holding to the truth God has revealed.

'It has given me great joy to find some of your children walking in the truth, just as the Father commanded us ... I am not writing you a new command, but one we have had from the beginning. I ask that we love one another.' (2 John 4-5).

Be Thoroughly Equipped
for the Fight

WE CONTINUE TO LOOK AT PASSAGES in the Bible which help us as a church to guard and uphold the teachings God has given his church. These teaching enable us to experience healthy relationships with Jesus Christ – so they are worth guarding.

2 Timothy is one of three little letters from Paul addressed to a church leader, in this case Timothy. These letters are to help the generation of church leaders in the time after the apostles, when people like Paul and the other apostles have died and are no

longer there to answer questions and offer oversight. Therefore they are particularly addressed to church ministers and church leaders in general and yet it is vital for every church member to be aware of them. They enable ministers to know what God expects of them, and congregations to know what they should expect of ministers.

At the very end of the letter Paul signs off, 'The Lord be with your spirit, grace be with you.' (4:22). This letter was originally written in Greek. In Greek you can tell the difference between whether a sentence is addressed to a group of people (in plural) are being addressed or just one individual. When Paul says, 'The Lord be with your spirit,' the pronoun is singular. This is because he is talking to Timothy the church leader. However Paul finishes with, 'Grace be with you,' and that final word 'you' is plural. That means Paul expected Timothy not only to sit quietly in his study and read this letter to shape his own priorities, plans and agenda; he also expected Timothy to have it read in the church congregation so that all of the church family could know what God wants from his leaders. The whole church family would have a vital role in supporting, upholding and encouraging the kind of leadership that God wants for his church.

We will come back later to that matter of what all of us as a church family should do to uphold the kind of leadership God wants in his churches. In verses 1-9 of chapter 3 we learn that we live in the 'last days.'

'But mark this, there will be terrible times in the last days.' (3:1) We think of the last days as being a phrase from a cheap horror movie. If we think the last days are real then we tend to associate them with strange esoteric goings on before the world is destroyed in a great cataclysmic event. The end times therefore are thought of by most as either fictional or future, but they are very real and contemporary. In Bible language and Bible thinking, the last days are the entire period of time between Jesus ascending to his heavenly throne after rising from the dead, in about 33 AD, and whatever time he chooses to return to his world.

The entire period between those two events of the first and the second coming of Jesus are the last days. So as God looks at his schedule planner the most important event he has in his diary after Jesus was raised from the dead is his return to this world.

It may happen next week, it may happen next year, it may happen in a million years; it does not matter. The entire period is called the last days. Paul was ministering in the last days, 100 years ago was the last days, we live in the last days.

As Paul is in prison, he writes to Timothy, his student and future church leader. The words to Timothy will in fact be for all subsequent church leaders who want to be faithful down through the centuries. They will need guidance and help, for 'in these last days in which you want to be faithful, there are going to be difficulties.' (3:1).

Paul lists some small words which describe the culture of people in the last days across the entire world. You can analyse the list by noticing the use of the word 'love.' It is instructive to notice what people love in the last days. Verse 2 states 'people will be lovers of themselves.' Later on in the same verse we read about, 'lovers of money.' Then in verse 4, 'people will be lovers of pleasure.' Lovers of self, lovers of money, lovers of pleasure and in the soil of those dark loves, many other weeds grow. Pride, boastfulness, disobedience to parents, a lack of thankfulness, a lack of forgiveness and slander spring up. The great, dark loves energise and shape every human culture and institution since Jesus rose from the dead until he returns. They are the world in which the Church must survive and to which it must be a witness.

So Timothy faces a massive temptation. If he wants to grow a great, successful church that people will love, all he has to do is organise it in such a way that it appeals to the love of self, love of money and love of pleasure. If you set up a church where people hear the message, 'You are wonderful and special – do not change anything,' it will grow. A church that appeals to love of self will be very popular.

If you tell people it does not cost much money to run a church they can be a member of, you can continue to spend all your money on yourself and whatever your pleasures are – such a church will grow as it appeals to love of money. If the church minister takes care to never challenge the worldly pleasures and sins of the culture, he will find himself presiding over a thriving popular church. A church which makes peace with lovers of pleasure will always be popular.

Many ministers build their ministries around

appealing to the pleasures of the world in these last days. Timothy is being warned to not take that route. As you read about the unpleasant sins of the world in these last days, it is tempting to think that Paul is writing about people outside the church, who know nothing of God or the Bible. Actually, the reality is much more frightening. The people who embrace these loves of self, money and pleasure and all these other unpleasant things that damage lives and relationships are inside the church. 'They are religious, they have a form of godliness but deny its power.' (verse 5). Is that not striking and scary?

In the last days there will be religious leaders in churches full of people who love self, money and pleasure. The leaders will look religious. The ministries will be successful. The messages will be popular. But the leaders will be manipulative and deceptive. Their appearance of godliness will be convincing enough to fool many – but it will lack the spiritual power that God grants all who love Jesus more than self.

Paul describes these leaders as 'the kind who worm their way into homes and gain control over people.' (verse 6). Also 'they will be learning and growing but they are always learning and never able to acknowledge the truth.' (verse 7). So you find these religious leaders always have further questions and further doubts to explore. They always have a new cultural perspective, something further that complicates what God seems to say in his word. Thankfully 'they will not get far because as in the case of the magicians who opposed Moses in the days of Egypt back in Exodus, their folly will be clear to everyone.' (verse 9).

To any church seeking to be faithful in these last days, Paul warns that, 'suffering and opposition are inevitable.' (verses 10-13). Suffering is an inevitable mark of faithful Christian ministry because in the last days there are all these behaviours and attitudes which set themselves against God and his words and anybody who is his emissary.

Remember Paul himself is in a Roman jail, chained up, awaiting his execution for causing trouble to the Roman empire by teaching people about Jesus. Paul is suffering but in this letter he urges Timothy to follow his example. However 'Suffer like Paul' is a message not just for church leaders. There is something inherent to the Gospel that means all believers will suffer in these last days.

It is wonderful that there are promises in the Bible; glorious promises that Jesus will give us life, that he will give us peace, that he will give us an entrance into the kingdom of heaven. These are treasured promises that we hold to and trust. But here is a promise from God that people are less keen to claim: 'In fact, everyone who wants to live a godly life in Christ Jesus will be persecuted.' (verse 12). Surely a promise that we find less appealing than others!

Every person who wants to live for Jesus wholeheartedly will face persecution and opposition, specifically because of their allegiance to Jesus. Can we cling to that promise? What does it mean for us? It surely means we must be extremely wary of anybody who suggests that becoming a Christian is merely going to make your life happy, comfortable and easy. Anybody who claims that the Christian life is pleasant in the way other ways of living are, is lying.

The Christian life can only be easy and comfortable if the message is deformed to appeal to those who love self, money and pleasure. Beware any suggestion that becoming a disciple of Jesus will be easy and just make everything in your life more comfortable. You are being invited to follow Jesus Christ who was crucified. Our leader suffered horrifically to bring us into God's kingdom. It would be most odd if the symbol of Christianity for Jesus our leader was a cross and the symbol for his followers was more of an arm chair with a nice cup of warm sweet tea! No, we follow a suffering king and we are invited to suffer as he suffered.

Perhaps I am one of the many who think of myself as a Christian simply because I come to church regularly? Maybe I know lots of things about God from the Bible or because I was raised in a churchgoing family? Yet, as I look through my life, I cannot put my finger on anything specific which is a difficult and painful experience which has come into my life because I follow Jesus. If I have not faced opposition specifically because I am committed to Jesus Christ, I need to ask myself, 'Am I really a Christian yet?' God says anybody who is committed to Jesus Christ will face persecution and opposition because of that commitment. It is an evidence of being a disciple.

Suffering for being a believer does not necessarily mean that you are in danger of being thrown into prison but it may mean a family member mocks you because of your commitment to Jesus. It may mean an awkward conversation at work when you tell people you went to church on Sunday morning or as you read your Bible on the train into work. Those little moments of tension and difficulty are evidence that we are following Jesus. Anybody who wants to live a real, faithful life committed to Jesus will face persecution. This is a promise in the Bible that we should believe.

As God's Church faces this kind of opposition, the leader of the church has to use the right 'equipment' to help the church family to keep trusting in Jesus. That is the message of verses 14-17. Timothy is told by Paul to in effect, 'Make sure you use the right equipment to support the church.'

I was chatting to a friend recently who bought a lovely new house nearby with huge wooden floors that have not been cared for over several decades. She has been crawling on the floor on her hands and knees sanding them down – with a little hand held sanding machine. She was telling me how uncomfortable it is and how sore her arms and her hands are from doing this physical work. I suggested to her 'Why don't you go down to the shop and hire one of the big upright machines like a hoover that you push around? Much more heavy duty – it is the right equipment designed for doing floors.' If she had been using the right equipment for the job she would not be in such pain, the job would be done better, everything would be more effective and quick. It is important to use the right equipment and the right tools in life. So Paul says to Timothy, 'If you want to look after the church family, if you want to help them keep trusting in Jesus despite persecution and opposition, you must use the right tool for the job: the Bible'. Look at verses 14 and 15.

'But as for you.' (verse 14). This is one of those great phrases of the New Testament. It underlines for us that Christian leaders are not to be wimpy conformists. Here is what everybody else is like Timothy but as for you, you have got to be different! You should be 'continuing in what you have learnt and what you have been convinced of because you know those from you who learned it and how from infancy you have known the Holy Scriptures which are able to make you wise for salvation through faith in Christ Jesus.' (verses 14-15).

Timothy was raised with some family members

who were Jewish, who knew the Old Testament. So Timothy was raised to learn the Bible his family knew. When the apostle Paul came along Timothy realised more fully that Jesus Christ was the Messiah promised in those Old Testament scriptures and he began to follow God more deeply and more enthusiastically.

You may have heard people talk about Christians worshipping the Bible. We are to value the Bible as God's word to us - but that does not mean you confuse the Bible with God! You do not worship a book but we should esteem the Bible greatly as the means by which we get to know Jesus. The scriptures are 'able to make you wise for salvation through faith in Christ Jesus.' (verse 15).

The scriptures are the tools which show us what Jesus is like, which enable us to trust in him, which correct our wrong views of God. Faith is nothing more than trust; relying upon something. We do not rely on things in life irrationally for no sensible reason. You are having faith in the seats on which you are sitting. I should warn you there is woodworm in them so your faith might be slightly misplaced but broadly speaking you are sitting on the seats because you have evaluated them and you feel that there is enough evidence they will take your weight if you sit on them. That is faith.

People think that faith – when it comes to Jesus – is of a different kind. So people often say that faith in Jesus is an irrational leap in the dark. That is not the case at all. Faith is an entirely rational, sensible response to what we learn about Jesus in the Bible. That is where the evidence is presented to us that he really is God, that he really did die to bring us into his kingdom, that he really is alive today.

On the basis of the evidence it is entirely sensible and rational to commit your life to Jesus even if it brings great opposition and suffering. The false teachers will not get very far but you continue in what you have learned and become convinced of. The tool then that Timothy is to use to look after the church, to grow people's faith in Jesus, to keep them pressing on through opposition, is the Bible. Like anybody keen for a student to use the correct tool to do a vital job, Paul gives Timothy a little lesson in how the tool should be used.

When you hire one of those impressive upright sanding machines you have use of a powerful tool – but you do need to read the instructions to know how all the different bits of it work. I have tried using one and without the instructions I would not know where to put the peripherals, how to hold it, which buttons to press or what speed to use. So Paul gives some instructions – a user's manual for the church leader, so that he will know how to use the Bible to look after God's people.

The first thing you need to know is what scripture is. 'All scripture is God-breathed.' (verse 16). Scripture: the words of the Bible. Paul explains to Timothy that he needs to remember that although these words were written by human beings, whether words in the Old Testament by Moses, or written by unknown hands, or words in the New Testament by the disciples of Jesus, 'God has breathed them out.'

Words are carried on our breath. When we speak we are inevitably breathing as well. As the words come out of our mouths they are carried on our breath. So Paul is saying the words of scripture, although written by humans, are nevertheless God-breathed. God has overseen the process so perfectly that with every single word they wrote, it is as if it has come out of the mouth of God himself. Every word is exactly what God wants it to be, which means there are no errors. Every word is the word of God, which means it has God's power to achieve exactly what he wants in our lives.

Scripture is God speaking. So if we want to hear God today we do not need to close our eyes and try to have a vision; we do not need to take drugs to have some sort of esoteric, out of body experience. We do not need to sit silently or wait making a funny noise in prayer! We just need to read the Bible, because the words of scripture are God-breathed. They are God speaking to Timothy and through those words, to us.

If somebody is to be a minister who looks after God's people, he has to be convinced that the Bible is the God-ordained tool for the job, and it is not merely a collection of human words, it is not merely our best reflections on what God might be like. Scripture is God speaking today.

When you are deeply convinced that the Bible is God speaking, then you can use it to do a number of different things that are necessary for the wellbeing of God's church. 'All scripture is God-breathed and is useful for teaching, rebuking, correcting and training in righteousness.' (verse 16). The Bible is for teaching. It is not meant to be locked away for the esoteric academics to complete doctorates on. It is for teaching every Christian for normal living day by day.

That is why we want in our church services to focus on teaching the Bible. We long to establish more and more churches and ministries that enable more and more Bible teaching. Teaching that brings people into contact with God speaking does not just happen in the pulpit; it can happen in small groups. It can happen with two people meeting together to go through a Bible study. It can happen with someone reading a book that is recommended from somebody in church.

The Bible is a book for teaching. A faithful church takes every opportunity to enable Bible teaching to occur. Each of the different ways of teaching the Bible has different strengths – we are wise to use the different forms of Bible teaching in ways that play to their strengths. So pulpit preaching is the kind of teaching that is best placed to share the heart of the Bible's message with the gathered congregation. Preaching emphasises spiritual power and application to the agenda of the whole church family. Small group settings are better placed to train people in Bible handling skills and offer a context for particular kinds of pastoral application and service. One to one Bible teaching enables a precision of tailoring the application to an individual that cannot be done elsewhere. Books are the best place to ponder detailed complex approaches that can be taken to the Bible's teaching. All of these methods have value – the good teacher will make use of them all in ways that make the most of their particular strengths. It is foolish to preach as if you are leading a group study, and it is unwise to preach when teaching one to one. Wise teachers will understand.

The Bible is a tool for 'rebuking' and 'correcting.' Let us not come to God thinking that we know everything! Let us not assume that the belief of our culture in these last days is what God says is right and is good. I wonder, are you prepared to let God tell you that you are wrong? Can you invite God to change your mind on a topic? Many today think they can be part of God's people but at the same time reject God's instructions on some area of life. It is part of the definition of being a Christian that I say to God in my heart, 'You are God; you know what is best, not me.' With that attitude, as I read the Bible I still find things that are difficult to believe, things that I do not like and insights that make life more problematic for me. Nevertheless I let God's word correct and rebuke me so that I might have a better relationship with the God that loves me and made me, correcting and training me in righteousness.

When you come across something in the Bible that you do not understand or do not like, rejoice! It is an opportunity to learn and grow in your relationship with God. If I have been reading the Bible for years and have never really come across anything I find difficult or unpleasant or that I struggle to accept, then how do I know that the God I worship is not just a projection? My idealised imagining of what God should be like? In other words, how do I know that my God is not basically me? It is so important to let the Bible correct, rebuke, train and challenge us. But doing so will certainly make us step out of line from our culture in these last days.

Through the Bible correcting our beliefs and changing our thinking, we find God grants us a genuine relationship with himself. Paul urges Timothy and indeed all of us, to not give up on Bible reading and Bible study. Keep encouraging church leaders to feed us with teaching from the Bible so that we can grow up more and more in relationship with him.

In the first five verses of chapter 4 we receive a great exhortation and call to arms from the aged apostle Paul. He is chained to the wall in prison but writes to Timothy, conscious that this is said 'in the presence of God and Christ Jesus who will judge the living and the dead and in view of his appearing and his kingdom.' With such a solemn sense of grandeur, Paul writes, 'I give you this charge.' (4:1). Here it is, the most important thing the Church must do.

What must it do? Give itself to poverty relief? Give itself to environmental concerns? Give itself to bringing peace on Earth? Give itself to propping up ecclesiastical building projects around the country? Issue a press release on the latest cultural tend? What is the Church to give itself to in these last days? 'I give you this charge, preach the word.' (4:2). Take the Bible, explain it to people, teach it, help them understand it, preach the word. When are you to do this? How high up the agenda is it to be?

There are many other good things people want

you to do and to focus on: Accounts, music, buildings, staffing, fund raising. Well, Paul gives us one thing at the very top of the agenda – he says 'preach the word.' And here is when you are to do it: 'in season and out of season.' (4:2). In other words, when people want you to do it and they think it is the right thing to do, you do it then. But when they do not want you to do it and they think that there is something more important for you to do, do it then anyway! In season and out of season.

I do not know for sure if Bible preaching is in season at the moment or out of season. I suspect it is out of season - but it does not matter in the slightest. We do it anyway, and we put it at the top of the agenda. Other good and valued things will be left undone – out of obedience to God. People may want to hear it or they may not – it does not alter our priority. Preach the word in season and out of season.

The Church Father Chrysostom, one of the great preachers of the early church, said, 'Let it always be your season and not only when you are sitting in church.' It is easy to encounter God's word in a church service; it is what we expect. But what about Monday morning? What about when we go to the family reunion later on in the week, or when we see that neighbour we find difficult? In season and out of season, when it is easy and when it is difficult, share the word of God with people.

It will be difficult since we live in the last days. Paul warns: 'The time will come when people will not put up with sound doctrine, instead to suit their own desires they will gather around them a great number of teachers to say what their itching ears want to hear. They will turn their ears away from the truth and turn aside to myths. But you, keep your head in all situations, endure hardship, do the work of an evangelist, discharge all the duties of your ministry.' (4:3-5). So you will be in a minority, you will be despised and misunderstood - but keep calm and carry on.

It is an incredible and terrifying promise. Churches will be led by so many leaders who will reassure and massage those captured by love of self, pleasure and money. Those who have ears itching to be told what they want to hear, will recruit such church leaders. They will find and pay ministers eager to go through the motions of doing church and religion, but who will basically tell people what they want to hear.

Paul urges Timothy to be realistic about the times and do not be like them. 'But you, keep your head in all situations.' (4:5) The false teachers are popular but they have gone mad. They may have gone insane, but you, do the sane thing – preach the word in season and out of season.

Use God's word to train God's people to trust in Jesus. Rather than making it easy for yourselves by giving into the culture, take a stand against the world and against the culture that opposes Jesus. Do this and you will have the crown of righteousness and glory that far outweighs anything else. As Paul did. 'I am being poured out like a drink offering. The time has come for my departure. I have fought the good fight, I have finished the race, I have kept the faith. Now there is in store for me the crown of righteousness, which the Lord will award to me on that day and not only to me but also to all who have longed for his appearing.' (4:6-8).

I know it is difficult and lonely in lots of ways, I know it can feel a thankless task now, but look ahead. In the future there is a crown. Jesus himself will welcome us into his kingdom. The goal of our church is to get as many people as possible ready for that day, and to keep going no matter what opposition comes. Your minister wants to do that. The second letter of Timothy is written to a leader and congregation – will you help me keep the right focus?

I know there are lots of good things we could do with our money, our time and our energy but let us give ourselves to the number one agenda item of sharing God's word with people. In a while our church will develop some fundraising, which we have not done for some time. Will you get behind the idea that we will raise funds to support the most important thing that God wants us to do? That is training and recruiting and equipping people to do more and more of this kind of word ministry at all levels in our church.

I know we can raise money to do lots of other things, good things, but let us focus on the top agenda that God has for his church: training and equipping people to preach the word in many different ways, so that more people come into God's kingdom. As we talk together as a church family will we encourage each other to spend time reading the Bible? Will we share with each other what we have heard from the Bible today that excites us or that challenges us? How encouraging it is when somebody says, 'I have had to change my mind on this issue because I have realised the Bible says something I did not like before or did not know before.' What an encouragement to somebody else in church to hear that over coffee. Will we ask God to make us into people who talk like that together as a church?

When Toleration
must not be Tolerated

Revelation 2:18-29

P EOPLE OUTSIDE AND INSIDE THE CHURCH have all kinds of very understandable views about what church is. It looks like a group of people who have gathered together for some kind of meeting or communal activity, and therefore it is understandable that we think of it as being some kind of social club – like a dining club or a guild or a football club. People choose to opt in if it is the kind of activity they enjoy.

Perhaps people think of it as some kind of a society with rules of membership and benefits and principles. Those rules and principles and benefits can be altered and changed if the members all get together and a majority of them vote through a resolution at their annual meeting. Or people think of the church as a group of people who are, in effect, committed to the preservation of beautiful historic buildings. All of those are very understandable views of what church is. Looked at from a human perspective, that seems to be exactly what goes on. But in reality church is far, far more than it appears to be.

Church is not merely a group of people who choose to meet together for a common purpose, with an agreement about what is right or wrong or what they are going to do together. Church is actually a group of people gathered together by Jesus to live for him in his world and to await his return. That being the case, what Jesus says about his Church matters supremely. Jesus knows and understands what goes on in his churches around the world and throughout time. His view about what we say and do is accurate and vital.

In the book of Revelation at the end of the Bible, we hear from John, the beloved disciple, that friend of Jesus who wrote John's Gospel and three letters in the New Testament. John has been exiled to an island as punishment for his refusal to give up on his trust in Jesus. The Roman state is threatened by the challenge that Jesus poses to them and so John has been exiled. While he is on this little prison island God speaks to him in a vision. God reveals to him what Jesus is going to do in the future and his plan and his desires for the churches.

There is symbolic language used in this book but it is a lot less weird and difficult to understand than people often realise. If you know the Old Testament, if you have read the Bible a bit, with careful reading of Revelation it makes sense. John has his vision and in Revelation 1:12 he says, 'I turned round to see the voice that was speaking to me. And when I turned I saw seven golden lampstands, and among the lampstands was someone like a son of man, dressed in a robe reaching down to his feet and with a golden sash round his chest.' John sees seven lampstands. They are symbolic. God is not really interested in furniture such as lampstands; they are symbols of something. The question is what are they a picture of? Well, the Bible is not as obtuse and mysterious as people might imagine. In the very last verse of

Revelation 1 we are told exactly what they mean: 'The seven lampstands are the seven churches.'

So, the lampstands that John sees represent seven churches. And in chapters 2 and 3 of Revelation, seven churches, real churches at the time John was writing, each get letters from Jesus. So these seven lampstands represent these seven churches. But as you read on you begin to get the sense that these seven churches represent not only themselves but all churches throughout all time. The message Jesus gives each of them seems to be exactly what he wants to say to us today.

Among the lampstands – that is among the churches – stands the Son of Man. That is Jesus' description of himself in the Gospels. The title 'Son of Man' is a picture taken from Daniel 7 and the book of Job. In Daniel it suggests a God-like person and in Job it highlights lowly humanity. So the Son of Man is one who at the same time exhibits both the nature of God and a human.

So John sees the Son of Man, Jesus. But before he sees Jesus he sees the churches; it is among the churches that Jesus stands. This reminds us that Jesus is not distant from his churches. He is present among them. He sees what goes on in them. He knows what they are doing. He knows their fears and their struggles: he knows their temptations and failures. Jesus knows what goes on in his churches. He is near them and among them. And it is this Jesus who communicates. He sends letters to his churches. And the one we are going to look at first is the letter to Thyatira.

These words come from Jesus: To the angel of the church in Thyatira write: 'These are the words of the Son of God whose eyes are like blazing fire and whose feet are like burnished bronze. I know your deeds.' (Revelation 2:18).

You see here that Jesus knows what goes on. The words of Jesus are also words from the Holy Spirit. The letter ends, 'He who has an ear, let him hear what the Spirit says to the churches.' (Revelation 2:29).

To the 'churches' plural because the church at Thyatira is representative of all churches throughout all cultures and all time. The letter could be written to our church. This is the Holy Spirit speaking. People say, 'I am wondering what the Spirit is saying to me today. I wonder what the Holy Spirit is going to reveal to me about God's plan for my life, or this problem that I have got.'

Well, here it is. The Spirit speaking to us today is telling us exactly what he wants us to hear. But we say, 'No, no. I want to hear about this relationship problem that I have got. I want to know about my career. I want to know about what is happening next year.' And the Holy Spirit says 'That's not what I want to talk to you about. I want to tell you what I want to tell you. Will you listen to me as I decide the correct topic that you need to learn about?'

But this is not just in the past, not just to this little church in Thyatira, the text is what the Spirit 'says'. Note the present tense. He speaks today to us, using the means which he has decided is the best way to speak to us – that is through a letter given to a church 2000 years ago which is now supernaturally used by God to speak to us afresh. The Bible says exactly what God knows we need to hear. It is remarkable! Who could have come up with a way of communicating with people so incredibly powerful and insightful, other than God himself?

What is it that Jesus says to our church today through the letter to Thyatira?

Jesus does not accept all toleration! A surprising message for us. Jesus does not accept all toleration. In verse 19 Jesus commends what is good about the church: I know your deeds, your love and faith, your service and perseverance, and that you are now doing more than you did at first.

What a positive start! What a compliment for a church! I know about your faith and service and you are doing more and more effective ministry and mission than you did in the past. What a splendid commendation! Praise God! And lots of us, because of our personality, temperament and culture, like to think of Jesus as only giving compliments like that.

But actually Jesus goes on to give a warning and a criticism. Remember that nobody loves the Church more than Jesus. He died for the Church. The book of Revelation describes Jesus as married to the Church as his bride. He loves and cares for our church, and therefore if he has something to warn us about, something negative to say, it must be because that is the most loving thing possible to share.

What is his criticism? 'Nevertheless, I have this against you: You tolerate that woman Jezebel, who calls herself a prophetess. By her teaching she misleads my servants into sexual immorality and the eating of food sacrificed to idols.' (2:20).

'You tolerate that woman Jezebel'. Toleration today is thought of as an unqualified good. It is always good to tolerate things; to tolerate people's opinions; to tolerate people's lifestyles; to tolerate people's choices. But Jesus wants to know whether the thing being tolerated is good or bad. Jesus does not accept all toleration as being good. He said, 'Tolerating this woman is a bad thing and I hold it against the church that does it.' Jesus calls her Jezebel. We do not know what her name actually was. Jezebel is actually the name of somebody in the Old Testament.

We read about her in 1 Kings 16. Jezebel was the wife of King Ahab in the Old Testament. Ahab was arguably one of the worst kings that Israel ever had in its history. He encouraged the worship of idols which brought with it sexual immorality into God's people. He persecuted the prophets who tried to bring God's word to Israel. He did all of this with the support and conniving assistance of his wife Jezebel. When people got in her way she invented false accusations against them to have them removed from the situation. I imagine we don't have anybody today called Jezebel – it is not a very popular name! Jezebel was a terrible woman who did great damage and harm to God's people.

So there is a woman in this church at Thyatira, who self-identified as a prophetess. In other words, she set herself up and was viewed by other people as a great religious leader who would tell people what God wants for their lives. But Jesus says, 'No. Actually I know what she is like and I warn you she is like Jezebel.' It is interesting that to understand what somebody is really like as a religious leader you have to look beyond what they appear to be. You have to listen to what Jesus says about them. And indeed, to even understand the meaning of what Jesus says about the religious leader, you have to know your Bible. The name 'Jezebel' means nothing if you do not know the story in the Old Testament.

People's opinions about somebody as a religious teacher, and the opinion that person has of themselves, and the appearance of a person may all be wildly out of step with what Jesus says about them. A church may even think it is being wise and godly by tolerating somebody's leadership. Jesus says 'You as a church tolerate this Jezebel and I hold it against you.'

Why in the Church today may we be tempted to tolerate religious teachers who are similar to Jezebel? Well, it is tempting to focus down and inwards on a tiny little part of life in the world. My little church is OK, my little life is OK, so what goes on with some bishop or church leader in another part of the country, hundreds of miles away is nothing to do with me. Such an attitude leads to toleration! We want to fit in with the world. Nobody wants to be unpopular.

The point is that people like Jezebel say things that fit in with what the world wants to say. So to not tolerate them brings us into conflict with the world that says we should tolerate all views. It is uncomfortable. We want to be polite, do we not? Many people have vested interests. In the Church there are leaders whose jobs and houses and pensions depend upon tolerating people's views. I myself am in that category actually. It makes faithfulness costly and difficult. We fool ourselves that the only thing God really cares about is the positive Bible teaching or ministry that we do. But that is not what the Bible says here, is it? There is no suggestion that all the people in the Church are acting like Jezebel and her followers. It is just that they tolerate her. Toleration of things that Jesus says are wrong is itself a problem. Jesus does not tolerate all toleration.

There is always hope. The people who follow this leader Jezebel will be punished by Jesus. They are described as her children, her followers. Nevertheless it is important to notice that there is always hope. They will be punished unless they repent. 'I will cast her on a bed of suffering, and I will make those who commit adultery with her suffer intensely, unless they repent of her ways.' (2:20).

Repentance is a Bible word that Jesus used many times, it's the heart of the response people make to the Good News that Jesus brought into the world. Repentance means a heartfelt turning away from sin, a deep inner change of direction in life. I used to be going one way, living for myself and doing what I want, trying to fit in with the world. I repent, I turn around. I walk in a different direction. The word literally suggests I change my mind and I go in the opposite direction. Jesus says that anybody who repents and turns around, will find a welcome and forgiveness. And this generous offer is even for these people that have followed Jezebel and done all the terrible things that she has encouraged. If they repent then Jesus will not punish them, he assures.

To say that Jesus accepts anybody as they are is really a half-truth. And it is a dangerous half-truth. Jesus will indeed accept anybody, but he proves that they are accepted by Him through changing them. The way we receive and respond to his loving acceptance, is repentance. Christians are people committed to change at a very deep, inner level of our beings. So Jesus promises, here and in many other places, that those who claim to be accepted by Him but who refuse to allow Him to change them, who in effect push him away by their lives; they will in the end be punished by Him for that.

It is significant that the issue at stake is not primarily the actions of Jezebel, but her teaching. There is no clear suggestion in the passage that Jezebel herself is doing anything particularly immoral. It is her teaching. 'I have this against you: You tolerate that woman Jezebel, who calls herself a prophetess. By her teaching she misleads my servants into sexual immorality.' (2:20).

By her teaching she misleads. Jesus spent his

ministry teaching people. The apostle Paul spent his time teaching people. It is very clear throughout the Bible that false teaching, messages about God which are half-truths or wholly untrue, leads to people living bad lives that God will ultimately punish. False teaching leads to bad living. And healthy good teaching leads to godly living. So God cares very much about what is taught in his churches. God will punish unrepentant leaders who teach things that lead listeners to live ungodly lives.

Today the Church of England finds itself under great pressure to tolerate teachings which are the views of the wider culture on various issues of life. So, for example, in one of the national newspapers this week, the MP of Lichfield took it upon himself to tell the Church of England what it should do. Presumably he feels the Government is doing such a competent job at governing they can focus on the Church as well as their normal portfolio of responsibilities!

He advised this: 'Perhaps if the Church's teachings were more in step with the population at large that would lead to more church goers.' So the assumption is that the Church should teach the same things that the population at large already believe. When people come into church for the first time they should hear the same kinds of messages that they find on the BBC news website, on Channel 4, or in the bestselling magazines, or from the parents at the school gate, from people who do not know God, who have never been to church and never read the Bible in their life. The views we should hear from the Church are exactly the same things as people hear elsewhere, and that would lead to a wonderful success for the Church.

No, according to Jesus in our passage that would lead to the Church tolerating teaching that is opposed to the teaching of Jesus. That would encourage people to lead lives in ways that anger God. Ultimately mimicking society would lead people away from God and to face punishment from Jesus. It would be a terrible thing. The Church should not measure its teaching by what the population at large already believes. The Church should measure its teaching by the teaching of Jesus Christ and his Bible. Jesus does not accept all teaching. Neither should his Church if it wants to be accepted by Jesus.

Eventually, **all churches will know who Jesus accepts.**

You see, today as you look around the Church it can seem unclear who exactly is on Jesus' side and who is not. The false teachers do not stand up and announce themselves and self-identify themselves as Jezebels or King Ahabs. No, they look like solemn religious leaders and teachers. And their followers do not as a matter of course openly parade the immoral living which is justified by the teaching of their religious leaders. It is in secret; it is quiet. And so today it is not always clear and it is difficult to know who is on Jesus' side in his Church, and who is not. Any false teacher who as a religious leader has responsibility for the wider denomination's leadership, puts in great effort and spends huge amounts of money on strategies to help them hide what they really do. But Jesus says that one day it will be made crystal clear who he accepts and who he does not.

'I will strike her children dead. Then all the churches will know that I am he who searches hearts and minds, and I will repay each of you according to your deeds.' (2:23).

The words of Jesus referring, I think, to his return to his world. At that time Jesus will judge his Church and judge the world. Verse 25 makes it clear: 'Only hold on to what you have until I come.' Jesus will return to his world in glory. And at that point he will punish those who have ignored his words in his Church. At the same time he will look after and comfort all those who have held onto his teaching.

Christians are people who look forward to the return of Jesus. We know that we cannot fix everything in this dark and tragic world, but we look forward to the day when Jesus will return and will right all wrongs. If we are looking forward to that day, we are looking forward to the day when famine is ended, when loneliness is ended, when war is ended, when poverty is ended, and when false teaching which leads people away from God is punished and ended. There is something way out of kilter with a church full of people who long for bad things to be stopped in the world, like famine and wars, loneliness and death, but who do not care one iota about false teaching being ended. Teaching which leads people away from God is a problem with which Jesus is pre-eminently concerned. It is most dreadfully serious.

Until Jesus returns things will be difficult. People will complain about our desire to guard faithful teaching and reject false teaching. They will say we are proud and fussy; old-fashioned and narrow minded. Well, it was difficult for John. He was exiled to a little island to live out his days in suffering and loneliness. But Jesus is both generous and realistic. He urges us: 'Only hold on to what you have until I come. To him who overcomes and does my will to the end, I will give authority over the nations.' (2:25).

Jesus does not expect us to do grand spectacular gestures. He does not expect us to fix things in the Church that he says he will not fully fix until he returns. He does not expect us to do amazing things beyond our capacity. Jesus knows how tough it is to go against the flow. He says, 'Just hold onto my word, keep believing me, do not tolerate this false teaching. Trust that I know best for you. Just hold on to what you have, and I will return and I will fix it. But do hold on till the end.'

There will be religious leaders who can look back on twenty, thirty years of faithful teaching, but now, in the latter days of their lives, they tolerate the teaching they once opposed. It is in some ways understandable – as people get older and approach retirement they long for an easier path. We need to see that Jesus says those previous decades of faithfulness are insignificant. Faithfulness only counts if you hold on until the end of your life. 'Until I return,' Jesus commands. A solemn encouragement to all of us to keep going to the end of life. It is how we finish that counts. We are weak, but if we will just cling to Jesus' words he will hold on to us.

I am committed as a church minister here to doing all I can to help our church hold to the teachings of Jesus, until Jesus returns. Will you pray with me and for me, that God will bless that endeavour? Will you help each other to do that by encouraging one another to keep reading his words? Keep believing and treasuring Jesus' words even if the world does not. Hold on to them even if many in his Church reject them.

Only the Weak can Win

Revelation 3:7-13

THIS IS THE FINAL SERMON IN A SERIES that we have been following over the last couple of months. We have been studying passages in the Bible which help a church to learn what it means to guard the teaching that Jesus has entrusted to us. We are conscious that there are many people who teach things in the Church which are contrary to what the Bible teaches. The Bible has lots to say to churches who want to resist that and want to hold firm to the teachings of Jesus Christ. Doing this is not an optional part of Christian faithfulness – it is one of the vital activities Jesus commands us to do.

We come now to a passage in Revelation which is a rich encouragement to all of us. It can seem like an insuperable challenge for a little church of people to hold firmly to the teaching of Jesus. God's word is unpopular and reviled in the wider culture. It is neglected and rarely defended by the senior leaders of the Church of England. I have sat in many meetings where bishops have explained to me that they view their role as not speaking out on the areas of teaching that people disagree over today. Were that the right approach for leaders to take, the Church would never have spoken about any topic! What can one little church do when faced with those kinds of challenges? Well the letter to the church in Philadelphia in Revelation chapter 3 is a great encouragement to us.

These letters in Revelation, we have already learned, are a series of letters that Jesus sent to churches through John, his disciple. John was himself suffering – exiled to an island as a form of punishment for his refusal to compromise on teaching the message of Jesus. The letters go to these seven little churches but actually we have seen they were for all churches. Somehow, in God's great plan, what he said to one of these churches is actually what the Holy Spirit says today in the present tense to all churches. You can see this in Revelation 3:7, 'To the angel of the church in Philadelphia.' But the message is not just for the church in Philadelphia because chapter 3:13 says, 'He who has an ear let him hear what the Spirit says (present tense) to the churches (plural).' The letter is not just intended for a church in Philadelphia two millennia ago. It is what the Holy Spirit is saying to every church, in every nation, in every age. This means if you are wondering what the Holy Spirit has to say to you today, it is in this letter. We may say to ourselves, 'I would like the Holy Spirit to speak to me about something else, about who I should marry or whether I should take that job promotion or whether I should move house.' But actually if we are going to show real respect to God, we should let him decide what he wants to speak to us about. And what he wants to say to us today is what he says in this letter. God speaks through the text to them then, to us today.

What is the first thing the Spirit says to us today? **Jesus guarantees our weak efforts (verses 7-8).**

We can be painfully conscious of the many challenges and forms of opposition – senior church leaders who set aside and do not defend the teaching of the Bible; a culture which opposes God at every turn; personal failures and struggles. So it is immensely encouraging that Jesus, who knows all that goes on in all of the churches, says, 'I know that you have little strength.' (verse 8).

It may be that you feel tired due to family commitments, due to work problems, due to age or health issues. It may be that looking ahead to the caring of a relative or a husband or wife in old age, you not know how it can all be done. Spiritually it may be that you feel that you have been let down again and again and again by family, by church leaders, or by friends. It may well be that you have tried to tell people how much you love Jesus and what he has done for you, and they just do not seem interested. Worse you find friends and colleagues do not want to spend time with you as they once did – you feel rejection for the name of Jesus. It hurts; it is wearying. So you feel weak. And Jesus says, 'I know that you have little strength.'

The one who both knew the mighty power of creating stars, and who also felt the weakness of human flesh as he died on the cross – this One says it to us individually and he says it to us corporately as a church family. We are just one little church. How could we have the strength to take forward God's mission in this world, with any real credibility and effectiveness? Consider all of the challenges and opposition that lie in front of us.

Jesus knows that we have little strength but astonishingly he guarantees our weak efforts. He uses the imagery of a door to get that message across to us. Have a look at verse 7: 'These are the words of him who is holy and true, who holds the key of David. What he opens no-one can shut, and what he shuts no-one can open. I know your deeds. See, I have placed before you an open door that no-one can shut.' Jesus says, 'I am the one who is in charge of the door. I have the key of David. It is invested with all of the authority of King David himself, the greatest king, the leader of God's people in the Old Testament.' Jesus is the one who decides when a door is open. If he opens it, nobody else can shut it. And if he closes it, nobody else can open it. Whether the door is open or not has no relationship to your strength – Jesus is the doorkeeper.

This image of a door, an open door, is used throughout the New Testament to describe new opportunities for mission and service in God's kingdom. In Acts 14:27 we read, 'They gathered the church together and reported all that God had done through them and how he had opened a door of faith to the Gentiles.'

The apostle Paul says, 'Because a great door for effective work has opened to me and there are many who oppose me.' (1 Corinthians 16:9), and also, 'Pray for us too, that God may open a door for our message, so that we may proclaim the mystery of Christ.' (Colossians 4:3).

There are other examples in the Bible. An open door is a picture of God himself opening a door for new opportunities for mission and service in His kingdom. The muddleheaded way we think is that we should not venture out into any new ministry or any new area of mission until we feel strong enough to do it. When we feel more capable and more strong, then we will move forward. So we feel we have to make sure we have hundreds of thousands of pounds in the bank before we venture forward in recruiting new staff or setting up new ministries. We need to wait until every seat in our church is full at every event we put on, and until there is a queue of people down outside the doors, before we begin to set up new ministries and new ventures. We need to wait until every spot on every rota is full of people and there's a waiting list before we set up a new ministry that requires new volunteers. You see the way we think naturally is that once we feel strong enough, then we can do something for God's kingdom. But if God allowed us to succeed like that, who would get the praise and the glory for work done in God's kingdom? It would be us. We would deserve all the praise for being strong enough to do it. Friends, that is not the way God works. A great door is opened by Jesus for new opportunities for mission. The door to mission is opened to the church that feels weak. 'I know you have little strength' (verse 8). That is the church to which Jesus says, 'I have opened a great door of opportunity for you.'

We have seen this already over the last few years at our church. To take an example, the Sunday Club for teaching young children. We have lots of children being taught about Jesus in little classes by teachers who are volunteering their time and making sacrifices in order to do that. There are so many children there that it is a positive experience for all. The teachers are enjoying it and serving well; when families visit for the first time and their children see what is going on, they enjoy it and they want to come back again. There are numbers of people here today that are here because your child enjoyed Sunday Club so much, and they nagged you and said we have to go to church on Sunday, get up out of bed! You see, it is a wonderful blessing; a great door has been opened for ministry there. But as I recall, at no point before that door was opened did anyone say as we discussed ideas, 'This looks like it will be very easy because we have got so many teachers willing to help and we have got so many people able to set up, and we have all the money to buy necessary equipment.' Nobody said those things and it never looked like it was going to be easy. We never felt we had the strength to do it, but in our weakness, God opened a great door of opportunity and has blessed us. That has been our experience.

Looking forward over the next couple of years, we've been conducting a review of women's ministry in the church. Will it be, possibly, that numbers of women who have not really been involved in any of the women's activities begin to say to each other, 'Let's all go along and join in and let's help this area of ministry grow and develop and be positive.' Could it be that occurs so much, that it becomes the kind of thing that people would invite their friends to who do not even come to church at all at the moment? Such a positive situation seems like it is a long way off. We seem to be far too weak to deliver that kind of vision. We do not seem strong enough to do that but surely it will be just like the Sunday Club – precisely when we do not have much strength, God opens a great door of opportunity and ministry to us.

You know that over the last year or so we've been talking with other churches in Tunbridge Wells about ways and opportunities and possible ideas about how we could set up new congregations around the area. We want to open up new doors for ministry and mission. Should we wait until it seems easy and we seem so strong that we do not really have to trust God? Or should we admit that we do not have much strength but we will venture forth anyway? As we do so we will ask that Jesus would open a door on our behalf. If we do all that with a due sense of our weakness, Jesus guarantees our weak efforts.

Secondly, **Jesus will show that he loves his faithful people (verse 9).** Over the last couple of months we have been looking at the painful, sad reality that there are many religious leaders in the Church of England and wider afield who deceive and lie. There are many who present themselves as great religious leaders and representatives of God but what they say falls far short of what Jesus teaches in the Bible they should be teaching. The image and the reality are very, very different from one another.

I know that when we begin to have our eyes opened to this it is very disappointing. Frankly, it is hurtful. As people begin to realise they have been giving money to organisations that have let them down; as people begin to realise they are willing to make real sacrifices to uphold the teaching of Jesus in their families and in their workplaces and in their personal lives; but the people they look to as an example cannot be bothered to lead by example. They are scared of what the media might say about them. They are scared of what their religious friends might say about them. They are scared they will lose some comfort and cultural acceptability. It is hurtful and deeply disappointing to realise that this is how it is in God's church.

So we need to see that Jesus says, 'If you hold

firm to my word, I will show you that I love you - not them.' It is shocking but see what Jesus says in verse 9: 'I will make those who are of the synagogue of Satan, who claim to be Jews though they are not, but are liars – I will make them come and fall down at your feet and acknowledge that I have loved you.'

We need to understand the imagery and the language of this passage. The assumption is that the Jewish people are God's people, they are his special people and God has loved them and used them to bring the message of Jesus to the nations. Satan is however, the great deceiver. He is the enemy of God who has brought sin and death into the world. Jesus is saying there are people who claim to be part of my family, part of my special people but they are lying. They look like your friends and supporters but they are playing for the other team. They serve not God, but Satan. Jesus said the same kind of thing, face to face with the religious leaders of his day. For examples, read passages like Matthew 23 and John 8.

We surely recognise that Jesus uses very strong language in verse 9. He says they are 'liars.' Such an accusation is not permitted in our parliament. But Jesus uses it. Jesus is saying in effect, 'Yes, I know you look like you are a church minister but actually you are a Satanist.' It is actually very similar to what Jesus said in John 8. It is definitely not the kind of thing that gets said in polite after-dinner conversation. Yet it is the language used by none other than Jesus Christ. This is a message Jesus has for his church.

Today in the Church of England some of the most ungodly things that are said and taught, are being taught by the senior leaders who should be doing the very opposite. To ministers like me and people in the churches who become aware of all this it is profoundly depressing. It is extremely hurtful. You feel let down, and rightly so. It is so helpful to know that Jesus is fully aware of it and he is going to bring to light what is hidden. Jesus is going to let it be made clear to all people who he thinks is doing the job properly and who he loves.

I was chatting to the chief executive of a hospital recently about malpractice cases- serious malpractice cases where someone is severely injured for the rest of their life because a nurse or a doctor did something wrong. He was saying to me that legally the hospital cannot apologise. The lawyers do not allow that. But this man was explaining that he knew from having talked to people in that situation, that while hundreds of thousands of pounds of compensation can be received, actually what people really want is an apology. When somebody does something really wrong and there are terrible consequences, we want it to be admitted to us and we want that face to face apology. That hospital director understood that. I think we all understand that very human need to feel that a wrong done to us be acknowledged. That is something people want, and understandably so.

Jesus looks at his churches and he understands that you have been let down by your leaders. He understands they have hurt you. They have failed to do what they should do. It is serious and Jesus feels it to be so. They have lied and have deceived. Revelation 3:9 says Jesus is going to arrange that face to face meeting where reality will be brought to light and apologies will be made. Jesus says, 'I will make them come and fall down at your feet and acknowledge that I have loved you.'

So today it may not be clear who is really doing a faithful job and upholding the teaching of Jesus. People may not notice that you have been hurt by false teachers in the Church. Rest assured that one day Jesus will arrange a meeting with those who have not done what they should do. They will be forced by Jesus himself to admit they served Satan. All will see what they were really doing and all will see who Jesus really loves. We wait for that day.

Thirdly, **Jesus will come soon – hold on till then (verses 10-13).**

'I am coming soon. Hold on to what you have, so that no one will take your crown.' (verse 11).

Jesus promises here, as he does throughout his ministry and throughout the New Testament, that he will come back to his world. Jesus came to his world the first time, two thousand or so years ago. We celebrate it at Christmas. He came in weakness; he slipped in unnoticed; he was hidden. Jesus allowed his enemies to nail him to a bit of wood and crucify him but he always promised that he would come back again. He assured us there would be a return to his broken world.

That second coming of the king will be very different to the first. It will not be in weakness, nor will it be hidden. It will be in glory and in power and in the visibility of all nations. Jesus will forgive any of His enemies who have asked for that. But there is a severe warning for those who continue to deceive, manipulate and rebel against Him. Jesus will punish them with a ferocity that is terrifying, described throughout the book of Revelation and elsewhere. Christianity is not just about the first coming of Jesus. We get the wrong idea if we think it is all just about remembering that God came to earth in Jesus as a baby and he loves his world and he died on the cross for us. All that is true, but it is also true he will return with glory and power and might, to punish His enemies and rescue those who have trusted in Him. Any genuine Christian has to let the sure and certain future return of Jesus shape their priorities and beliefs. The future return of Jesus must impact our attitude to false teachers in the Church. We need to reject the idea that false teaching does not matter – the future return of Jesus ensures whether people have taught rightly or wrongly about God matters immensely.

Christianity is not even just about information in the Bible about Jesus. It is about far more than that. It is about the reality that the real Jesus is actually coming back. He is coming back to his world. That the date is in God's calendar, that it is approaching, changes everything. Jesus says, 'I am coming soon'. (verse 11). What he means by that is that his coming back to the world in glory and power and might is such a significant event, that it makes everything else pale into insignificance by comparison. The return of Jesus will be so momentous that though it has not happened yet, it changes today and it changes tomorrow.

How does the return of Jesus relate to these great doors of opportunity for mission and service being opened to a weak church? You could think to yourself that if Jesus is coming back and it could be tomorrow, then none of that is of any relevance. There is no point me making any great sacrifice to serve Jesus today or to try and do a new ministry or mission. Why should we work and plan to set up a new congregation to reach a different area with the good news about Jesus? Why should we do all that work and effort if Jesus might come back next week anyway? Why bother?

The point is that we are supposed to be living in light of Jesus' return, knowing it could come at any moment; but it is as we are waiting for Him that we work for him. We work for him because we know and believe he is coming back. It's like the office worker who's been told they're going to have an important meeting with their boss. The office worker is told to go into a meeting room and wait for their boss to come in, sometime after lunch. The office worker is sitting there waiting; they know the boss will text them at any moment to say, 'I will be with you shortly.' Their phone is on the desk and they keep glancing at it wondering when the text is going to come. 'I wonder what he is going to say to me about last year and what are his plans for the future?'

The worker is looking for the text message, waiting for the phone to buzz. But as they sit in the office waiting for that text message to say, 'I'm just round the corner and I'm coming in now', their computer is on and they're working at the spreadsheet of financial returns. The employee knows that when the boss walks into the office, he will want to see that the employee has been busy doing something useful. We work as we wait.

It is difficult work. We are surrounded by those who do not believe that Jesus is coming back. We are surrounded by religious leaders who are not what they appear to be. But it is precisely when we feel weak; it is precisely when false teachers seem to have the upper hand in His church; it is precisely at that moment Jesus says to his churches, 'I have opened a great door of opportunity for you. Step through it. I will be with you. And if it is painful and difficult, press on – I will be back soon. I will take you to be with me forever.' Let us pray that when Jesus opens those doors of opportunity to our weak little church, we see the open door for what it is. May we step through it. May we feel weak enough that we are driven to depend on Jesus. And when Jesus returns may he have all the glory.

CPSIA information can be obtained
at www.ICGtesting.com
Printed in the USA
LVHW111537170619
621475LV00001B/366/P